What people are saying about

Others

Martyn Percy offers us a feast of common wisdom about our life in the world with others. In conversational tone he narrates stories, beliefs and experiences that touch the breadth and depth of human experience and point us toward the God-given gift of one another. An engaging and accessible read for the inquiring spirit, personal reflection and group discussion.
Steve Pickard

This delightful and insightful book is a short read with a long reach. It challenges with wit, scholarship and humility many ingrained views of 'Others' who hold differing beliefs and disbeliefs.

Stimulating Percy theology at its finest.
Jonathan Aitken

Tread carefully as you open this book. It is a life-changing piece of writing — whimsical, profound, endearing, moving, personal, informed, insightful, and wise. It is a book packed with holy insight written for everyone. Martyn Percy at his best and most stimulating.
Ian Markham, VTS

This is not an easy book, but its topic is demanding emotionally, intellectually and spiritually. To get traction on 'otherness', you need both an expanded framework and the willingness to think differently. In a condensed way which is ideal for group discussion, Martyn Percy opens many doors and dodges no issues. He writes from the heart and is uniquely qualified to do this.
Iain Torrance

Others

A Very Short Book About Beliefs

Others

A Very Short Book About Beliefs

Martyn Percy

CHRISTIAN ALTERNATIVE
BOOKS

Winchester, UK
Washington, USA

JOHN HUNT PUBLISHING

First published by Christian Alternative Books, 2023
Christian Alternative Books is an imprint of John Hunt Publishing Ltd.,
No. 3 East St., Alresford, Hampshire SO24 9EE, UK
office@jhpbooks.com
www.johnhuntpublishing.com
www.christian-alternative.com

For distributor details and how to order please visit the 'Ordering' section on our website.

ISBN: 978 1 80341 068 5
978 1 80341 069 2 (ebook)
Library of Congress Control Number: 2021949991

A CIP catalogue record for this book is available from the British Library.

Design: Stuart Davies

UK: Printed and bound by CPI Group (UK) Ltd, Croydon, CR0 4YY
US: Printed and bound by Thomson-Shore, 7300 West Joy Road, Dexter, MI 48130

Contents

For
Deborah, Dominic, Mark, Peter, Suzanne, Kate, Henrietta and
Simon
Jonathan, Alan, Nigel, Henry and Deborah
Catherine, Sarah, Alex, Brian, Andrew, Keith and Emily
Andrew, David, Alan and Martin
and other pilgrims
with much gratitude for your care, counsel and kindness

Feast of Epiphany, 2022

1

Introducing Others and Beliefs

Thank you for picking this book up. I almost decided to write this anonymously, as the name put to it could cause some readers to prejudge the text. And since the book is essentially about the prejudices and beliefs we all have, I hope you can see my point. That said, this very short book is really just a long essay, and designed to make you think outside the box. And here I assume you might accept that most of our thinking takes place in all kinds of boxes. These boxes have labels, such as 'class', 'gender', 'culture', 'plausibility', 'impossible', 'imagination'; and 'faith', 'fantasy', 'fiction' – and most sacred of all, the box we usually label as 'facts'.

I hope you will enjoy reading it, and I should say at the outset, I really don't mind if you are religious or not, or class yourself as spiritual but not religious; or are open-minded, or quite closed-minded (and proud of that). Or for that matter a happy, grounded atheist. Or a grumpy one, come to that.

I've written this book about beliefs because I think we don't really understand other people and what they believe. And that in the twenty-first century, this is rather startling, and possibly quite disturbing. And that if we understood people better, we might have an easier time of it in our local and national politics. In our international politics, for sure. In our churches and communities, and in our societies. And maybe in our neighbourhood. Just imagine Ned Flanders and Homer Simpson getting along well.

I know people can believe strange things. Perhaps you know some people like this too. Or maybe you are one of the people I think are strange, or just 'other'. I like the fact that the traces of this alterity – funny word, that, but just academic-speak for 'otherness' – lives on in our language. Take rhubarb, for example. It is a vegetable, but most commonly treated as a fruit. Its texture – only the stalks are eaten – is much like celery when raw, although the plant is more closely related to sorrel.

The ancient Greeks thought all foreigners sounded alike, and had an onomatopoeic word for them: 'barbarians' was derived from the sounds that Greeks supposed foreigners made when speaking. Literally, 'Bah, bah bah, bah...', which has survived as a kind or synonym for senseless word salads in our own time: 'Blah, blah, blah...' *Barbaros* was the Greek word for foreigner, and *rheum* means 'flowing, stemming of discharge'. For rhubarb was a foreign plant, probably first imported through Russia from Tibet and China (where it was known as the red-yellow plant – nothing if not descriptive!). The obvious medical term that is linked to this is rheumatism, from later Latin *rheumatismus*, meaning to 'suffer from the flux or flow', as our ancient forebears thought that rheumatism was a natural discharge from within the body that caused the pain in the joints due to the excessive flow of *rheum*, which made the muscles and ligaments stretch and ache. People do believe strange things.

'Barbarian', as a term, has survived in the English language to a remarkable degree. The first meaning of 'stranger' means 'from another country'; 'outlandish', likewise – from the outlands. Alien meant 'from somewhere else'. It is an intriguing feature of the early Christians that they were pro-alien, very welcoming, and strove to be inclusive. As a consequence, they became outcasts, and were driven out of the synagogues they worshipped in. So they looked after outcasts and aliens just like themselves. That said, rheumatism can be a pain like no other, and of course, only you will have that pain. No one else can feel your pain for you.

I'm an Episcopalian (or Anglican) priest, and an academic. So I have encountered a fairly broad bandwidth of beliefs within the denomination to which I belong. I've met some who think Calvin was the best thing since sliced bread. Others who think Calvin (and Hobbes) were interesting thinkers but can't really see what they have to do with the church, while others smile knowingly, and enjoy meeting people who like a good cartoon strip that involves a small kid and his toy tiger that is only actually alive when the adults are not around.

I've met others who are very sure about the incarnation, resurrection, and other beliefs. They can be quite dogmatic. I've encountered others who are very unsure about these beliefs. They can be quite dogmatic too. And I have met many conservatives, liberals, Catholics, Evangelicals, and others who don't like labels, but are up for low, middle, and high church, sometimes all in one day.

I don't know about you, but quite a lot of people I know can be quite muddled, or change their minds a bit, or have beliefs that they believe in strongly one day but just a tiny bit less the next. I know people who had beliefs and lost them. Or threw them away. Or could no longer carry them – so they dropped them because they were too heavy.

I've known others who think they had no beliefs before, but now have a lot of them after... and it is usually a conversion, trauma, Damascus Road experience, or some such. Others I have known have swapped beliefs, in much the way that an ardent fan of soccer or basketball might someday support one team, and the next, switch affiliation. This can be costly for them, because if you switch your support, you can lose friends and family. You might gain new friends and family. But sometimes people who change allegiance lose everything they held dear. Sometimes this choice alone is too much to contemplate, so they just drop out – like leaving high school or dropping out of university. 'This belief thing wasn't for me,' they say to themselves. It happens in religion, politics, and with the rules of an association or society, and those boring, tiresome people you might meet at some local club. It can happen with almost anything. Supporting my football team and hoping for their success is an exhausting and utterly fruitless experience. And yet I believe...

Beliefs are funny things. Do they define us? Or perhaps they choose us? Or do we go and select our favourites, and get to define ourselves? I recall a near neighbour of mine, decades ago, who kept a posh fancy tea service in a nice cabinet (i.e., the real deal – bone-china cups, saucers, plates, etc.), because she was convinced that when Jesus returned, he would call on her for tea, and she wanted to have the right crockery for that moment. She never used this tea service for anyone or anything else. She did occasionally show it to friends and explain what its use would be. As it turned out, she died, and so she never used it at all.

Was this crazy? Perhaps. But she wasn't. She was kind, caring, attentive, prayerful and reflective. But she did have a thing about Jesus, tea and cake. (I never had the courage to ask her what kind of cake she thought Jesus might actually like when he returned – she made a good Victoria sponge, but I always felt her fruit cake was below par. I never asked her what tea Jesus might like either – Darjeeling? With milk, lemon...? But I digress.)

I once took a funeral for a woman who was devoted to her husband, and he to her. He had liberated her from one of the Nazi concentration camps at the end of the Second World War. He was a young soldier, barely twenty-one. She was thirteen. Never mind what you think about the legality or appropriateness of this relationship. Go back to the start of this paragraph. She was a young adolescent in a concentration camp, without parents or siblings – an orphan, courtesy of Nazi extermination. She was alone in the world; no family survived. They fell in love and married as soon as they could. They had children and were happily together for over sixty years. When he died, she was convinced that he continued to live in their house, and it made her so happy. She evidenced his continued life very simply: the toilet seat was often left up, and that indicated he was in the house, using it, because he would stand to take a pee. He tended to return when she was out shopping or chatting with neighbours.

I'm an academic as well as a member of the clergy. I was interested in fundamentalism, and it was curious to encounter various reactions to my research. Some people just assumed that I must be an ex-fundamentalist. Others suspected that I was really still a fundamentalist, and somehow trying to justify all those weird beliefs that fundamentalists are supposed to have. Fundamentalists that I did meet as part of my research looked at me pityingly, witheringly, or took a couple of steps back, in case they caught some kind of contagion.

I remember interviewing one ardent Revivalist, who told me that Jesus could heal anyone of anything, any time. Even the dead could be raised: anyone, any time. I'm a curious person by nature, so I asked, 'Well, what kind of dead person?' They looked at me, puzzled. 'What on earth do you mean by that?' they exclaimed. 'Well,' I said, 'what about someone who is cremated, and has their ashes scattered at sea?' 'Don't be ridiculous!' they retorted. (I must confess, I thought I had really crossed the line here between satire-sarcasm or even insulting them.) But then they added, 'Of course! Jesus can do something with those ashes! Where is your faith?'

Christians of all kinds have beliefs that we might think odd. Do healing miracles really happen at Lourdes (France), Knock (Eire) or Medjugorje (Croatia)? I imagine if you think they do, they might. Which is not to be casually dismissive of causality. All I am saying is that most, if not all, humans have hopes and expectations, and to some extent, we will reap what we sow. Our social, political and spiritual constructions of reality are personal, shared and communal, and also temporal and cultural. Muslims in Kyrgyzstan still undertake pilgrimages to the shrines (*mazārs*) of Solomon's Mountain, where they seek cures from sacred trees and attach prayers, blessings and invocations to the branches with colourful pieces of cloth. For many Muslims, this is Bad Islam. But I suspect that for most Protestants, and quite a number of Catholics, the mere mention of Lourdes, Knock or Medjugorje will prompt a change of subject, embarrassed silence, or an unwelcome tirade of corrective doctrine.

In previous centuries, our forebears have believed in magic, spells and superstition. How many of us, seriously, don't at least register row number thirteen on a flight or floor number thirteen in an elevator? How many of us are not at least slightly curious about the horoscope we flick through in the old magazines as we wait for the dentist? When my father-in-law died unexpectedly in his home, I was the executor. Discussing this over lunch one day with friends and colleagues from China, they informed me that the property was now worthless, as it would be occupied by a ghost. In fact, one of the surprising recurring statistics in China is the number of pedestrians killed each year when stepping onto busy roads – many of whom, it seems, genuinely believed they were evading a ghost. (And yes, the ghost can get run over too, though I don't have any sense of how we can know that.)

The Christian Bible tends towards condemning magic and magicians, but the difference between miracles and signs, and magic is, well, debatable. Yes, some miracles are for healing. But others are clearly attention-seeking, or even bizarre. The Koran refers to magic (*sihr*) over sixty times. Magic is not something that is 'all in the mind', so to speak, but it does need a social construction of reality – or a plausibility structure – in which to 'work'. Otherwise we would not notice it. Only when you have been conditioned into normality (whatever you think that is) can you begin to entertain the supranormal, or the supernatural.

There is, of course, a dark side to this – evil, witchcraft and Satan (or the Devil). Here again, we have the history of ideas that have taken on particular guises over time. Few of us today would see heresy as evil, let alone linked to witchcraft. Some of our forebears saw it differently, and the punishments and executions for such alleged trespass were frequent and severe. Various Pentecostal and Charismatic Christian groups have invested in colourful and variegated demonologies, with prayers for exorcism ranging from the short and instant to the extensive and prolonged. In 1980 *Michelle Remembers* became a bestselling book. Co-written by Canadian psychiatrist Lawrence Pazder and Michelle Smith (one of his psychiatric patients and, later on, his wife), the book relied on the discredited practice of recovered-memory therapy and made lurid claims about satanic ritual abuse that contributed to the rise of the satanic ritual abuse moral panic in the 1980s.

Much of the Charismatic, Pentecostal and Revivalist fervour of the 1980s was indebted to these new (or in fact, rather old!) social constructions of reality, and in the USA, Canada, New Zealand, Australia, Israel, the UK and Europe, multiple cases of ritual abuse suddenly began to 'surface'. In 1993 the British government reported on eighty-four separate allegations of satanic ritual abuse. Despite extensive investigations, no credible evidence of any secret satanic circles emerged. Despite numerous claims of aborted foetuses in rituals, or even of infanticide, no bodies or human remains were uncovered. In some respects, we have now come to see what I term 'the return to Satan' in the modern era as a sign of our inability to cope with evil, failure and neglect.

The anthropologist Jean La Fontaine advised on the 1993 report, and took the view that it was still easier for people to attribute neglect and harm to demonic or satanic explanations when it came to trying to understand the mistreatment of children. In other words, we moderns were still minded to externalise our inner fear, disgust and loathing, and map this from a spiritual cosmology rather than one that was political or social. That is not to say, of course, that the reconjuring of evil amounts to merely primitive superstition.

On the contrary, as the philosopher Mary Midgley noted, the growth of administrative cultures throughout the world makes it much, much easier for individuals to surrender themselves to the powers of evil. The Nazi Holocaust is a particular example of one kind of mass group surrender to multiple layers of administration, and of the banality of evil. Someone designed the camps; others fitted them out; others built the railway tracks and others drove the trains. Others still designed the ovens, and others made the uniforms. To effect this, never forget the sheer amount of administration involved – the timetables, the paperwork, the names and numbers, the need to reach targets for deportation and transition. Each and every cog – a person – in this administration machine was 'just doing their job' and 'obeying orders'. Our social and political structures are riddled with this, as are churches. We don't need a real Satan at all. We just need to be realistic about the evil that systems can cause or camouflage.

I don't have a view on whether you think these views are dotty, quaint, serious, silly, or stone-cold sober and solid. I am interested in how we look at the beliefs of others, and why this matters today. I want to invite you to think differently (and perhaps more humbly) about the beliefs you have – what you think you are reasonably sure of (or, if you are a Calvinist-loving, Conservative-Evangelical Anglican, feel free to substitute 'reasonably sure' with 'absolutely certain' – if you'll feel more comfortable that way). Because how we regard beliefs is how we regard others, and these folks are our neighbours, and that matters. It matters what they think, and so we need to be smarter in our understanding of them, if there is to be a better 'us'. I invite you to think differently about your neighbour, and all those others, and what you think they believe and do but probably don't…

2

Disbelief and Unbelief

One of the little-known facts about the rise of early Nazism relates to the professions that were most represented in the rank and file of the party and movement. By several furlongs, the answer is: academics at German universities and colleges. You may think that is shocking enough. But be prepared for the aftershock: many academics were also members of the clergy. Why and how, you may ask, could this be so? After all, the Nuremberg trials revealed horrific war crimes on a scale not witnessed before or since. Surely to God, intelligent academics and kind clergy could not have been party to this? But think again.

The conditions for the rise of Nazism were economic, social, ethnic and political. The psychological conditions are arguably harder to name: shame, guilt and terror at the humiliations of the Great War and its aftermath. And then the social self-preservation kicking in, which invested in old myths to justify the flexing of new moral righteousness. We forget that most card-carrying Nazis were on a *moral* crusade. And like all crusaders before them, they had demons to slay, enemies of God to slaughter, and huge investments in scapegoating. The Turks, infidels, Armenians, Jews, gays and others – all can testify.

How was such certitude about the Jewish pogrom expressed at Nuremberg, seventy-five years ago? It depended on who was on the stand. Some were certain that they were right, and happy to meet their fate and suffer the consequences. Others sought salvation through that oft-repeated trope: 'I was only obeying orders.' What Nuremberg showed the world was what Hannah Arendt was later to describe memorably as 'the banality of evil'.

More on banality in a moment. But before then, older readers may recall the numerous scenes in the final episodes of BBC TV's *The World at War*. (Younger readers are encouraged to visit YouTube to watch, as the programmes were made fifty years ago.) Or the recent footage that has come to light of the Allied forces liberating the death camps. The Allies often found the camps deserted by the guards, with piles of unburied corpses, ashes, ovens and emaciated people starving to death. How did the Allies respond to the sights and traumas that they were witnessing, and that would haunt them for the rest of their lives? In many cases, they rounded up the local populations near the death camps, and made them walk through, and look at what their compatriots had done. Where there were no neighbouring death camps, the population were herded into cinemas and made to watch newsreels evidencing the atrocities. Only after sitting through a screening were viewers given their ration tokens, stamped, for bread. If you did not see the death camps, it was hard to come by food.

Most people might assume that faced with the shock, trauma, and reality of the death camps, they might, in Old Testament terminology, 'rend their hearts and garments'. Some did. But if you watch grainy old film footage of townspeople walking through their local neighbourhood death camp, marshalled by Allied troops, you see other reactions too. Some hold their heads high and look away – a proud, almost haughty posture, as though somehow they have been confronted with 'fake news' and odious Allied propaganda. Others stand and stare, and weep in disbelief.

Others walk past slowly, as at a funeral. Some run, fleeing from the very sight (and site). A small few remonstrate with the Allied troops at the showcasing of such a grim spectacle. It was nothing to do with them, after all. The reactions in the German cinemas were the same. Some fled in terror. Some scoffed. Others sat in utter, total shock. Some went home and took their own lives. For many years after, the suicide rate among German women was the highest in Europe. There is only so much a witness can take.

The classic study of cognitive dissonance and religion – for that is what we are dealing with here – is Leon Festinger's 1956 epic, *When Prophecy Fails* (Festinger, Riecken et al 1956). Less well known is Festinger's distinctive articulation of 'social comparison theory', namely the premise that people have an innate drive to accurately evaluate their opinions and abilities, so seek to evaluate their opinions and abilities by comparing them with those of others.

This is important in the church – and always has been – as Christian groups like to say what they are most *like* (comparison), but equally, that they are special, so *un*like anything else. This will produce distinctive grammars and cultures. So, in terms of safeguarding, the Church of England has 'core groups' – but not like anything else you can find on any other planet. Clergy have 'annual appraisals' too, but again, not like anything else you can find on any other planet. The church runs all kinds of systems that *sound* as though they will be comparable to their secular counterparts. They never are.

Festinger had a distinctive take on cognitive dissonance too, and at its most basic, his hypotheses went something like this. The existence of dissonance (or inconsistency), being psychologically uncomfortable, will always motivate a person to try to reduce their dissonance and achieve consonance (or consistency). When dissonance is present, in addition to trying to reduce it, the person will actively avoid situations and information that would likely increase the dissonance. Disbelief and unbelief are not the same. To refuse to be confounded is different from refuting faith in the face of contradicting facts.

On this basis, flat-Earth fanatics, QAnon followers and believers in the immortality of Elvis will always be with us. QAnon's far-right conspiracy theory alleged that a secret cabal of Satan-worshipping, cannibalistic paedophiles was running a global child sex-trafficking ring, and were plotting against former US president Donald Trump while he was in office. QAnon is commonly labelled a cult. Nothing you can say will contradict a truly devoted believer.

Festinger and his colleagues noted that every time you provided reasons to disbelieve, this led to an *increased* conviction in beliefs. Such beliefs were always held with deep conviction. These beliefs produced actions or validated realities that were impossible to undo. (So, if the Bible suggests the world is 6,000 years old, well, it is, and science, geology and palaeontology can't undo that 'fact', because – and don't forget – this new-fangled empiricism and knowledge is *younger*.) All attempts to refute beliefs will only *intensify* and confirm those beliefs.

This also explains how, when people were being rescued from, leaving or escaping from the inferno of David Koresh's compound outside Waco in Texas in April 1993, they didn't thank their rescuers – who were paramedics, police and other emergency services – pulling them out of the burning fires. No. Those being rescued quoted scriptures, especially Revelation. Those rescued were already interpreting their furnace and the deaths as a scriptural fulfilment. Their time was at hand. They might well have been escapees from the fires of this life, but they were more concerned with remaining faithful to the prophetic calling imbued into them by David Koresh, and so more concerned about avoiding the eternal flames. That is why, I guess, they even tried to evangelise their rescuers on that fateful April day.

But let us return to our German audiences in 1945. By making populations and communities *see* and be forced to bear witness to what had been done in their name, what did the Allies hope to achieve? Cynics may say it was vengeful: passing on the trauma the liberating soldiers had endured to the people who had been sitting with this right under their noses for several years. I am not sure, however, that this is fair. Nuremberg was, after all, about education. It was an extended enterprise in accountability, responsibility and justice. It was a way of holding a mirror to the world, and to all of us, and saying: *Look and learn*.

The banality of evil is commonplace. 'Banal' means 'common,' 'ordinary' and 'shared'. Arendt's phrase gets right under the skin of what communities, societies, groups and churches find to be so utterly normal that they cannot see its actual evil. Racism, sexism, abuse of all kinds: these are part of the ecology of churches. We have just got so used to this stuff. We no longer notice it. Moreover, this is not innocent, as, indeed, beliefs are not in themselves. One person's belief can be another person's oppression. Or liberation. Or enslavement, and perhaps annihilation. Wars are fought with words, ideas and beliefs, and are not just about some narrow squabble over material capital.

We might imagine that wars are determined by key battles, and struggles between right and wrong, and good and evil. But they are essentially about resources (i.e., material, human, information, etc.) and territory (i.e., perhaps land, but more often social, political, ideological and moral capital). Wars are about who has the right to might: the power and position to assert or will-to-power. War is a political and moral venture, but one that utilises industry and resources on a vast scale to achieve its ends. To lose a war is not so much about losing a fight as it is about the right to determine one's future, and this, in part, explains why wars are so costly and bitter: they are utterly existential.

But war shocks others. And when they see it, they are furious. Their anger can be uncontrollable. You can understand perhaps, just a little, why, when Allied soldiers found camp guards hiding among the concentration camps, mercy was in short supply. The murderous rage that the liberators felt might be in all of us, somewhere. Most of us react to evil with shock – and also disbelief. We cannot believe that what we see and hear has been said and done. How could others say or do such things, we ask? Where some see processes in which people are 'only obeying orders', we find ourselves unable to comprehend our devastation, despair and alarm.

The banality of evil is contagious. Where it occurs as a pattern of belief and action, it is akin to a Bad Surprise. The Catholic theologian Clemens Sedmak says that one of the primary tasks of theology is to see it as an invitation: to wake up – to be mindful and attentive. Black Lives Matter has a slogan: 'If you are not angry, you are not paying attention'. Quite. This is what the Allies did with cinemas and walkabouts in 1945. It was a powerful poke in the eye: *wake up* – just *look* at what has happened! Yet some still could not see, and would still refuse the lesson. It is hard to make people learn who are not willing to be curious. Certainty can often be the enemy of truth, for just that reason.

Alas, I never met Robert (or Bob) Towler, who passed away in 2020, aged seventy-seven. Bob wrote a fascinating sociological treatise called *The Need for Certainty* (Towler 1984), in which he explored the different ways people can be religious within the conventional traditions of the main Christian denominations. One might say that Bob's life contained a degree of oscillation. Bob's father was a barber in Norfolk and used to visit Sandringham to cut the hair of King George VI. As a young man, Bob joined the Community of the Resurrection, an Anglican religious community for men based in Mirfield, West Yorkshire. While there, he studied for a degree in sociology at Leeds University and left Mirfield in the early 1970s to become a sociology lecturer at the same university. In 1974, Father Hugh Bishop, who was then the Prior (i.e., head) of the Community of the Resurrection at Mirfield, resigned his position and set up house in Yorkshire with Bob as his partner. They were very happy together. After Hugh died, Bob met Sarah Toynbee in 1989, who was working in publishing at the time. Bob retired from his post (by now in broadcasting), and he looked after their two children, Fred and Maddie.

The Need for Certainty is a clever little book in so many ways, because it analyses the beliefs of others. It is based on in-depth analysis of letters sent to John Robinson, then Bishop of Woolwich, after the publication of his 1963 bestselling book *Honest to God* (Robinson 1963). What Towler does with great economy and flair is to describe and label five contrasting ways of being religious.

The five are:

1. Exemplarism
2. Conversionism
3. Theism
4. Gnosticism
5. Traditionalism

Towler explores how, despite these five being mutually incompatible, they can coexist in the churches, and in individual believers. In doing so, he argues that a proper grasp of this wide variation in styles of religiousness is a prerequisite for quantitative surveys of religion. Each contrasting religious style is explored in turn and illustrated with quotations from the original letters. Being a proper sociologist of the second half of the twentieth century, Towler understands intense desire for religious certainty, and it is this that is extensively explored – and ultimately presented as a debased but common form of religious aspiration that often leads to the degeneration of faith. Certainty can often lead to intransigent fanaticism – so is the very opposite of faith. It makes no room for doubt, and has to be asserted.

If I am right about the moral purpose of the Allies in 1945, or of Black Lives Matter now, then the obvious thing to say about the primary task of education is that it is not – and never was –

first and foremost about pumping out information and dogma. No. It is about arousing curiosity. If the educator cannot ask 'why is it like this?', or 'does it have to be that?' and 'could it not be better?', then Jesus was wasting his time with parables and miracles.

Education matters because it is inherently political. Always. It cannot avoid the human condition, and our social understandings of ourselves and of others. Black Lives Matter is pedagogy, not dogma – it seeks to teach us to look, and to re-examine our basic assumptions and presumptions. Just as Nuremberg tells us to stop being so blind, deaf and dumb. It is a call to the world to wake up. Someone should have asked where the trains were going with so many people in striped pyjamas. In the same way, we should be asking why so many BAME people die in police custody, or are in our prisons, or are arrested. The answers are seldom comfortable. But comfort is seldom your friend. Of that we can be reasonably certain.

Curiosity leads us to searching: to self-search; to probe; to wrestle; to change; to repent; to risk; to love; to sacrifice; to empower others; to be responsible; to see, judge and act; to be accountable to one another. I don't know about you, but I don't see any of this in our governments, societies, communities or even our churches and their approach to the injustices and inequality they continue to perpetrate. Instead, I see and hear leaders saying: 'This is just the way it is at the moment'; 'We are on a learning curve'; 'We are on a journey'; 'We are doing our best,' and, 'We've come a long way.'

Those in power must begin by setting aside their power, and repent of seeking control in the lives of others. We can only be moral by working together in a spirit of genuine reciprocity. An overconfidence in the ability of one group to initiate good for another always carries risk. Namely, to deny that other capacity – the one that causes unintended harm. It reflects a dangerous assumption on the part of those in power: that only *their* injection of goodness and morality can reform society and liberate others. Countless impositions of initiatives on racism and sexism suffer from this. And now safeguarding. Lies are more common in silences than words, says Adrienne Rich. Authentic listening has to be the starting point.

Seventy-five years ago, some people were traumatised by what the Allies showed them. Some looked and then turned away. Those on trial had just been running a process and had the right moral reasons for doing so – or so they thought or told themselves. The banality of the evil was that no one running the processes or obeying the orders exercised any moral courage or leadership. And so the pogrom continued. Because the cognitive dissonance was always in place.

Theology is an invitation to wake up. Not just to believe things. But also to be ready to disbelieve too. It is about honesty and authenticity. By this, I mean that we have to own up to what we ascribe to God, and how we think we describe God. Because no Christian has ever seen God, everything we have to go on in relation to God is essentially someone else's description (which we might find reliable, because it is in the Bible, or the Pope said it, or our elders or bishops make a statement), and our instincts and experiences, and our ascriptions. We can also say that religion does not just teach you what to believe, but also what to disbelieve.

3

Thinking Inside and Outside the Box

I guess the most obvious kind of box for the mind is to treat yourself as a prisoner within it. But this is a sentence from which there is no remission. You can't be released from your mind. True, people speak of 'losing their minds', but in fact they don't ever lose them. They only get lost in them. I reckon we get lost in our thoughts most days. But your thoughts are yours, and while you can share them with your friends and neighbours, and even publish them like this, they are your thoughts, and they are therefore most at home in you.

This is not as hopeless as you might think. In truth, we are locked in an endless oscillation of the cruel and the kind, and these cogs grind away within us in a movement of slow circularity. The outcome of our individual and collective thinking – the reward-punish axis, our fear-fright-flight-fight impulses, the rescuer-victim-persecutor triangle, to take some modern psychotherapeutic paradigms – is to invent the prison. Here we can dispose of deviants, but we don't entirely eliminate them, because we need their prolonged (or even perpetual) punishment to be a reminder that debt, deviance and acts of destruction must be paid for. Indeed, atoned for. Moreover, this means prisons hold up a mirror to society, and remind us of what human groups and societies will not tolerate within themselves.

Michel Foucault talked of the prison as a 'carceral system' – process-orientated project-managed persecution that weeded out dissident thoughts and dissenters. For Foucault, prison is a term for one part of a vast network of 'boxes' inside which people 'think'. These boxes include, but are not limited to, schools, military institutions, hospitals and factories, which build a panoptic society for its members. Foucault reckoned this system creates 'disciplinary careers' for those locked within its corridors. If you dare to dissent, you can be punished.

Edward Said's work as a cultural critic deconstructs and critiques coercive and corrosive Western ideas about the East, or the 'Orient,' which the West considers as 'other', or as the 'uncivilised' counterpart to the 'civilisation' of the West. (Said used this term in constructing his ideas, but academics tend not to deploy it now, and rather counterpoint the Global North and the Global South.) Said's most famous work, *Orientalism* (Said 1978, which coined the eponymous term), takes apart the false assumptions made by Western cultural production about countries in Asia, North Africa and the Middle East in particular, and explains how they function to perpetuate imperialist and colonialist ideas, to the ultimate benefit of the West and at the expense of the East, in a pattern of imposing essentialising and reductive binaries that strive to separate these imagined territories.

His work traces a line through initial studies of the 'Orient' by Westerners as a way to gain understanding and familiarity with culture, to how this was and continues to be used to subjugate the objects of their study, and how Western culture strives to intellectually justify this. By 'othering' and finding alterity in the East, Orientalist studies reductively looked to erode the nuances and diversity of regions, homogenising them purely as the opposite of the West, and characterising them as irrational and unenlightened. In his words:

the limitations of Orientalism are ... the limitations that follow upon disregarding, essentializing, denuding the humanity of another culture, people, or geographical region. (p. 108)

His work focuses on how these harmful ideas affect individuals excluded from and undermined by the power of Orientalism, and looks to 'widen the field of discussion, not to set limits in accord with the prevailing authority'. He argues that the imperialist mind-set gained its power through the disenfranchisement, degradation and alienation of non-Western subjects – the figure of the 'subaltern'. As such, Said is a figure that holds authority to account in responsibly shaping discourse, and to avoid the production of ideas that frame the East inaccurately. Part of this is his insistence that we examine the temperamental and easily influenced conditions of this framing:

> To build a conceptual framework around a notion of Us-versus-Them is, in effect, to pretend that the principal consideration is epistemological and natural – our civilisation is known and accepted, theirs is different and strange – whereas, in fact, the framework separating us from them is belligerent, constructed, and situational. (Gregory 2004, p. 24)

This is intriguing, because the territory of 'temperament', we are in swampy terrain, and not on terra firma. We as human beings are individual and collective spaghettis of impressions, rules, codes, stories, facts, myths and feelings. And much of what survives in us as adults, whether in groups or alone, are shared memories. They shape our beliefs. Most of us will react with flight, fight and fright when faced with trauma, danger or tragedy. What soothes us will invariably enable us to be more empathetic, and certainly to function better morally and socially. Few of us cherish our traumas, unless they serve our vigilance in flight-fright-fight mode.

Much of this is rooted in experience, but some of this can develop deep roots in our felt-senses – our feelings. As the writer and poet Maya Angelou says, 'I have learned that people will forget what you said, people will forget what you did, but people will never forget how you made them feel.' I think she is right. But it isn't true, either, to say we are 'nothing other than feelings...' (to paraphrase Morris Albert's 1975 lyrics), and it is actually quite difficult trying to 'forget any feelings of love' we may have had – because they tend to be remembered with fondness or regret, and anyway leave some scar tissue on our heart and soul, and even our flesh. What one is tackling here would be recognised by Foucault:

> Truth isn't outside power, or lacking in power ... Each society has its regime of truth, its 'general politics' of truth: that is, the types of discourse which it accepts and makes function as true; the mechanisms and instances which enable one to distinguish 'true' and 'false' statements; the means by which each is sanctioned; and the techniques and procedures accorded value in the acquisition of truth; the status of those who are charged with saying what counts as true. (Foucault and Gordon 1980, p. 131)

As Steven Lukes, the political and social theorist, has perceptively noted,

> conceptions of power may be divided into two very broad categories. On the one hand, there are those which are asymmetrical and tend to involve (actual or potential) conflict and resistance. Such conceptions appear to presuppose a view of social or political relations as competitive and inherently conflictual ... On the other hand, there are those conceptions which do not imply that some gain at others' expense but rather that all may gain: power is a collective capacity or achievement. Such conceptions appear to rest on a view of social or political relations as at least potentially harmonious and communal. (Lukes 1979, p. 636)

Lukes suggests the possibility of power relations that are 'harmonious'. Foucault, however, encourages a hermeneutic of suspicion. So at the heart of these issues of abuse, power and polity, there are some key questions. How does truth speak to ecclesial structures of power and polity? What would constitute a good 'theory of reception' for the churches in relation to the pain of those who have been disempowered by abuse? How should the churches initially receive the raw, un-pasteurised anger of victims, when it is directed back towards the manifest abuses of power, practice, trust, role and identity perpetrated by the churches?

Language is important, I suspect. How does the abused person 'speak' truth to power structures, exactly? Here, the philosopher and novelist Ursula Le Guin makes a helpful distinction between 'mother tongue' and 'father tongue'. The 'father tongue' is the language of power: 'spoken from above ... it goes one way ... no answer is expected or heard...' (Le Guin 1992, p. 149). Now, this is a 'labelled' way of thinking, for sure. But it might help us connect to othering and beliefs.

So, why do some things make *less* sense, yet somehow ring *true*, and 'feel' *authentic*? Why do some facts sound 'wrong', even though they appear to all add up? Anyone who has listened to propaganda, or indeed generated it (as, I confess, I have done in an earlier career), for example, a PR person explaining away a disaster by a person or organisation, will already know that we can feel that we are being lied to, even if the words and account are logical. This matters for us, because feelings locate themselves in our bodies and minds, and they gain an authenticity and currency that has a value. And sometimes that value is greater than the seemingly insurmountable facts. Anyone who has 'fallen in love' – please note the use of the word 'fallen' here – will have some experience of losing their rational senses and being caught up in a much deeper set of truths and beliefs, even if they can't be easily explained. Falling in love is an experience of helplessness; even as we tumble and stumble, and finally fall, we cannot stop this. Now, later or, perhaps, ever.

St Paul had a pretty good crack at explaining his new-found faith, but I am never entirely sure that he quite grasped the significance of his Damascus Road conversion. Equally, I am not sure it matters to us, or mattered to him; it takes a whole lifetime to become a Christian. The new paradigm he emerged in could not be explained easily. But it had trumped his previous one, and he simply could not deny it.

Le Guin gives us two modes of thinking about belief and emotions, and they are related. The 'father tongue' is the clinical language of the lecture theatre or the professions – it distances the emotions, passions and desires. In contrast, the 'mother tongue' is the language of the home. It is, according to Le Guin, 'inaccurate, coarse, limited, trivial, banal ... earthbound, housebound, common speech, plebian, ordinary...' But for Le Guin, the 'mother tongue' is also the language of connection and relationships; its power lies in uniting and binding, not dividing. It is Le Guin's contention that much public discourse, especially professional discourse within institutions, is a learned 'father tongue' that deliberately marginalises the realm of feelings and the scope of relationality. She argues that a recovery of 'mother tongue' within public discourse is an essential step for the reconstitution of public life, where 'plain' speaking can reclaim its proper value (or currency) as *bona fide* expression.

It is often the case that in relationships where the expression of anger is denied its place, resentment festers and breeds, and true love is ultimately distorted. Strong feelings need to be acknowledged for relationships to flourish. If strong feelings on one or both sides have to be suppressed for the sake of a relationship, then it is rarely proper to speak of the relationship being mature or healthy. In cases where sexual abuse has taken place, or some other abuse of power within the church (say on matters of gender, sexuality or another 'protected characteristic' in law), the church often seeks the compliance of the abused, and rarely censures the abuser. Gentleness and love that is detached and self-sacrificing have often been held up as the virtues that Christians should be striving for. Sometimes civility and peaceableness are paraded as ideals or archetypes for ongoing communion.

Now, civility is certainly an important virtue in the church, but often with little acknowledgement that the *form* and *patterning* of polity has normally been established by those in power, so that, consciously and unconsciously, their privileges are maintained. At the same time, we may need to appreciate that anger and aggression are often correlated with violence and chaos, and their intimate connection with love is therefore not acknowledged. The expression of passionate feelings, or perhaps of any feelings, is seen as a threat to the polity that maintains the power of an emotionally detached rational faith. The danger, as two feminist theologians, Beverly W. Harrison and Carol S. Robb, point out, is that:

> We need to recognize that where the evasion of feeling is widespread, anger does not go away or disappear. Rather, in interpersonal life it masks itself as boredom, ennui, low energy, or it expresses itself in passive-aggressive activity or in low moralistic self-righteousness and blaming. Anger denied subverts community. Anger expressed directly is a mode of taking the other seriously, of caring. The important point is that where feeling is evaded, where anger is hidden or goes unattended, masking itself, there the power of love, the power to act, to deepen relation, atrophies and dies. (Harrison & Robb 1985, p. 15)

Equally, aggression is almost always understood as negative, and often equated with violence. Yet feminist writers such as

Kathleen Greider call for a proper reappraisal of aggression and its place. She points out that the Latin etymology of 'aggression' lies in the verb *aggredi*, meaning 'to move towards', and she uses an intriguing working definition that is significant for our discussion here. Greider sees aggression as a central part of human nature present from our earliest infancy. It is as important as love in the human capacity to survive and thrive:

> aggression is one primary expression of the life force, of the drive to survive and thrive, embodied in positive and negative movement toward and engagement with goals, persons, objects, and obstacles ... These two primary forces can be seen in infants who have at birth both the sentiment (love) to engage others and the force (aggression) especially through their ability to cry, to influence the powerful others around them to meet their needs... (Greider 1996, p. 125)

Thus, for Greider, aggression and love are interrelated. They are both deeply connected to the importance of building and sustaining relationships that enable self and other to flourish:

> When functioning in this essential unity, aggression and love cannot be fully differentiated. However, an approximation of their particular contributions might be that love is 'desire' and aggression is 'movement' ... Aggression enables love to move toward the thing desired, love enables aggression to desire the thing toward which it moves. Love has gumption in it, aggression has affection in it. Without this intermingling, love might be passive, aggression might be only self-serving; with this intermingling, aggression is more likely to be constructive, love is more likely to have [the power of good]. (p. 127)

This working definition of aggression alters our perception

of the term. It relocates it as a neutral given in human and organisational relating that can be expressed positively and negatively. In its positive form it is about drive; about the activity that moves things forwards so that love and relationships might flourish. In its negative form, it reacts with violence to those things that appear to deny or destroy the self and their core. Thus, 'aggression is used negatively when it is directed toward wasteful and or unconscious violence; aggression is used positively when it is directed toward the affirmation of life and well-being in both its personal and collective dimensions' (p. 129).

Greider's 'aggression' is what others might call 'assertion'. The feminist writer Celia Hahn writes that 'assertion means moving outside oneself, reaching out with vigor and initiative, acting on the world' (Hahn 1994, p. 21). Hahn draws a clear distinction between aggression and assertion, seeing the former as negative, but Greider argues that sometimes it is the very strength of aggression that is needed. She reflects on the fact that on the rare occasions where aggression is defended by an aggrieved or angry person, it is because it is often justified on behalf of others or constitutes a creative push. So what is needed is a reappraisal of aggression for the sake of self, and the value of its destructive as well as constructive power: Greider talks of the possibility of 'creative destruction' (Greider 1996, p. 133).

As Lytta Basset noted in her *Holy Anger: Jacob, Job, Jesus* (Basset 2006, pp. 70ff), Jesus does not repress his own feelings of anger that can often spiral up within us and find expression in insults and other forms of aggression. Instead, Jesus' condemnation is of a more distant kind of anger: that which treats another as a 'fool' or as 'mad'. Because this kind of labelling refuses to meet a person face to face, it consequentially maintains the inner violence we feel, since the possibility of an appropriate or equitable relationship is now severed. As Basset notes, strikingly, Jesus does not say 'you have no reason to be angry', nor does he investigate whether the anger is justified or not. Rather, what matters is what is done with this boiling rage. So, Jesus appeals to us to turn to the other person: the object or subject of our wrath. Hence, we are invited – indeed implored – not to offer a sacrifice or gift until there can be some kind of reconciliation with that other. Only then can the sacrifice be liberating.

We are starting to encroach on some fairly familiar Girardian territory. The anger that we have and feel must be purposefully directed and responsibly communicated. It cannot be hurled at those we feel might merit our fury. As René Girard explains,

> Instead of giving back more of the same, we must leave the matter at hand to the potential rival. That is the unique role of the Kingdom ... To protect themselves from their own violence, humans ended up channelling it towards innocents. Christ does the opposite. He offers no resistance. He does not devote himself to sacrifice in order to play the sacrificial game, but to put an end to sacrifice... (Girard and Gregory 1995, p. 76)

Jesus does not refute or oppose the anger of the abused or marginalised. Nor does Jesus deny his own anger, or soft-pedal the anger of God. Instead Christ invites us into his relationship with God the Father, which does not model competitive desire, thereby providing us with a pattern that does not have space for mutual destruction. This allows Basset to argue that holy anger is therefore *not* an appropriation of God's anger 'in the divine mission against others' (Basset 2006, p. 210). For God's anger is something altogether other than human anger. Rooted in judgement and love, and in the overcoming of idolatry and injustice, God's anger is a positive and purposeful force that always seeks justice and peace. Indeed, the quest for perfect love, says Basset, must always pass through anger (see Basset

2006, pp. 263–4). Parents know this for sure; children too, though it takes time.

So, discovering how to acknowledge and give voice to raw experiences following abuse – in ways that can enable radical working together for the growth of all – is a challenge that the churches need to heed. In his ministry, Jesus listened to the voices of the marginalised all the time. He was receptive to their pain and sense of isolation, incorporating such voices into his ministry. Jesus made the marginalised his central concern, and placed those who were used to being at the centre of attention out to the periphery, thereby reordering society, forcing people to witness oppression and the response of the Kingdom of God to despair, anger and marginalisation. In our communities, institutions, churches and denominations, we need to allow the experiences of the oppressed and abused to challenge and shape the way we hold power and broker relationships.

Thus, the churches need to continually learn from the veritable panoply of liberation theologies: that marginalised people should not simply be made welcome in the church, but that their (raw, unrefined, 'mother tongue'?) anger and aggressive desire for justice might be allowed to reform the polity of the church. Learning to listen to narratives that convey strong, powerful feelings and experiences of abuse and marginalisation, rather than seeking to dismiss such stories as 'uncultured' or as 'bad grammar', is a major and costly task for ecclesial polity and pastoral praxis. Ultimately, the aggression of those who seek justice may help the churches to move on from their 'tamed and domesticated' valuing of crucifixion and suffering for its own sake, and work instead for the abused: 'not to perpetuate (more) crucifixions, but to bring an end to them in a world where they go on and on...' (Harrison and Robb 1985, p. 19).

I am more than conscious that an argument for an institution – which could be a small one like a family, or a congregation, college or assembly of some kind, bound together by filial ties or shared values – and in which raw and angry experiences of abuse and marginalisation are allowed to be given their full vent is potentially dangerous and irresponsible. We are all well aware that there is rightful place for reticence, and for the withholding of emotional speech. All of us understand that a temperate ecclesial polity can depend on finding a non-emotive language for expressing views and communicating across divisions.

However, I am also struck by how many kinds of bodies, polities and institutions deliberately disenfranchise and marginalise the proper expression of feelings and experience. Moreover, they have developed 'soft' and 'coded' structures for asphyxiating such speech, and pasteurising raw, strong, vernacular language. I find this not only to be poor emotional intelligence, but also humanely and socially weak and urbane, rendering the group or institution into some kind of semi-detached pasteurised-homogenised realm, in which all the correct probity of politeness and a polity of civility are observed, but 'real' feelings and experiences are never mentioned or aired. This just represses anger, often turning it into boiling rage.

How, though, do we discern when anger is a legitimate call for justice, and when it is a petulant reaction to simply not getting one's own way? Here we need to look at patterns of power and the motivation of anger. If you are a Christian, the good news of the gospel is partly about the accessibility of God: the welcoming in of the religiously marginalised, and the breaking down of barriers. So, in any kind of aggression and anger, we need to be clear whether it constitutes a move towards a vision of the Kingdom of God (or *kin*-dom of God, as Mujerista theology has it – Mexican-feminist-womanist theology that resists machismo, male violence and domination), and how it is motivated by the radical mutuality of love.

The command to love God and to love our neighbour as ourselves ultimately defines the place of our aggression and anger. It demands action, and that action demands drive, which at times requires generative anger and aggression. The church needs to find a way of holding and utilising the strong feelings that are part of human loving, remembering, as Harrison and Robb put it, that 'the important point is that where feeling is evaded, where anger is hidden or goes unattended, masking itself, there the power of love, the power to act, to deepen relation, atrophies and dies' (Harrison and Robb 1985, p. 15).

Part of the ministry of Jesus involved the expression of anger and was occasionally constituted in acts of wilful aggression. It is hard to imagine some of Christ's words being spoken in anything other than simmering rage. There can of course be something like a *creative* rage – the kind of rage that the poets and the prophets speak of – which is markedly impolite, but utterly godly. The task for the churches, therefore, is to find ways that do not suppress or block out strong feelings of anger, or hurt and the aggression it arouses, but to help discern how to channel the energy they bring into the work of the gospel.

So all of this means listening to the experiences of abuse and marginalisation that have led to aggression and anger and seeing them as far as possible from the perspective of those with less power. It means humility on the part of those who hold power, and an acknowledgment of the fear of losing power and control. It means a new way of looking at power relationships that takes the gospel seriously. It means churches and church leaders getting in touch with our feelings and developing an emotional intelligence – the kind that can lead to a new kind of ecclesial intelligence. And this, surely, is what we want from our leaders. People who can receive and handle feelings – even strong ones – and sometimes communicate the same when necessary.

It is under such circumstances that one can begin to conceive of the possibility of 'truth speaking to power (structures)'. For this speech to happen, the power structures and framework of the institution must be both robust enough and sufficiently humane (i.e., compassionate and empathetic) to understand that a 'theology of reception' requires churches to receive coarse, vernacular and strongly articulated feelings. This means thinking that is supple, sensate, serious and incarnated through its proper forms of human engagement. It needs to be thinking that is comfortable with the thoughts it feels, of which love could (or should) be primary. Love is reckless and risky, but also calculating and careful. I can teach it, and I have certainly learned it. But I have yet to attend a course that tutors me in the ways of love. It is odd when you think about it. This is the most essential aspect of being human. But this is a course that lasts a lifetime, and from which no one ever graduates.

So, in considering others, think of love. The feelings and experiences of others cannot and should not be silenced or pasteurised as a precondition of receiving your care – and their right to justice. Where care and justice are denied, societies and the churches have a prescient vocation and task to foster 'loyal dissent' until such time as we are faithful to the 'we' that makes 'us'. For Christians that is found in being faithful to the incarnation and vocation of Jesus – namely, to be the feeling, seeing, hearing and sensing body of Christ that proclaims the Kingdom of God. A moral and social Kingdom of Politics, moreover, where righteousness may reign. One of justice, human dignity and equality, and collective renewal, justice and restoration.

4

Other in Words, or in Other Words

It is funny how often 'other' appears in other words. Few of us speak of 'pothering' these days. It means to put someone into a pother, and in so doing flustering, worrying or perplexing them. Pothersome people are bothersome people: they make a fuss and they make us fuss. We don't speak of 'fothering' much – unless one is nautically inclined, as it means to cover a sail with oakum, rope yarn, or other loose material, with the view of getting some of it sucked into a leak, over which the sail is to be drawn. Generally, we don't like being smothered. Or for that matter, being over-mothered. Most of us have views on who is a good soother, and who is a good smoother in situations.

The truth about beliefs is that they can be perplexing when we encounter them. Moreover, like people, we never fully understand them. And that includes the ones we think we believe in ourselves. Nobody can fully explain themselves. So we have a hard task on our hands to even try and manage a decent explanation of someone else. It can be all a bit, well, baffling. Now, take a word like 'baffling', and we find that this word originated from one of Captain James Cook's explorations of the lands of the south: Australia, New Zealand, and the like. The *Oxford English Dictionary* faithfully records Cook's name alongside entries for 'taboo', 'tattoo', 'albatross', 'cannibalise', 'chocolate', 'gun', 'mangrove', 'mockingbird' and 'kangaroo'.

The thing about other people's beliefs, and quite often of people in general, is that they are baffling. But what did Cook think 'baffle' meant? Although the word originates from a Scottish sixteenth-century term that means to expose someone – particularly for perjury – the nautical term was adopted by Cook to work out how to sail directly into a headwind that would make straight sailing well-nigh impossible. The word 'baffle' meant to course a strange or fittingly unpredictable path – zigzagging or spiralling or some such unexpected motion – in order to make progress. Therefore, what baffles us now is people, thoughts and ideas that are not straightforward. We seem to move in contrary ways that to others are, well, illogical and odd. Baffling.

I write as a parent, but also as a child who has been parented, and at some stage or other we will all come across this exasperated question: 'What on Earth were you thinking of when you did that!??' The question can be asked in anger or sorrow – it doesn't matter which. But essentially we're asking: what on earth do we think the other person believed they were doing, and had they thought for a single moment about the consequences of their actions?

I happen to think that Wittgenstein had it right when he said the best thing that philosophers can do is give each other time. Jonathan Haidt in his remarkable book on moral philosophy meditates on this fact in his book *The Righteous Mind*. He reflects that he conducted an experiment at Harvard in which one group of people were asked to make a moral judgement on a particular issue, and another group were only asked to make the judgement after two minutes of time had elapsed. Inevitably, people who take time tend to make better decisions and have greater perspective (Haidt 2012, p. 81). It would seem, therefore, that the connection between time and belief is quite an important one. The things I believed passionately in my youth, whether that was a folly of love or an infatuation, get ironed out over time, and only by allowing ourselves this time to reflect will we begin to understand our own inner emotional terrain just a little more.

There is an incredibly interesting and teasing essay by Marilynne Robinson written in 1994 titled 'Puritans and Prigs'. Robinson gets to grips with the shorthand way in which we tend to think. To use the word 'puritans' is a barely polite economic term for describing someone who we think of as priggish or prudish, and possibly bordering on fundamentalism. Certainly, we imagine that such people are invested in a form of ,tightly-controlled and narrow framework of belief and so, by our reckoning, not thinking very well. Robinson quite rightly invites us to think again and look more deeply at the terrain of what is in front of us. Things are never what they seem (Robinson 1994).

Invariably, the more you investigate any human being or community, you find variations of belief, passions and practices that suggest something far richer and broader in tapestry than the convenient headline we have used to dub the group. For example, Pharisees and Sadducees mean something to most Christian readers of the New Testament. We equate those two groups, who are quite different, with a particular attitude towards Jesus, and a particular attitude towards the law of Moses. It's hard to say if any of our views about Pharisees and Sadducees are right, although we know enough about Nicodemus to at least be reassured that some were curious and enquiring.

T. S. Eliot authored an essay over a century ago about a particular phenomenon that he thought was a product of our advanced capitalism, perhaps emanating from the Reformation and the increasing availability of cheap printed materials. Eliot's essay said that if there was so much to be known, and there were so many fields of knowledge in which the words are used with different meanings, everybody ends up knowing a little bit about a lot. It therefore becomes increasingly difficult for anyone to know whether they know what they are talking about at all. You don't have to venture far in politics or economics to know this is the case. Indeed, it is exactly this kind of phenomenon that gives birth to the strange theories that revolved around Donald Trump's presidency. He could be the person chosen by God to eliminate a satanic paedophile ring. It certainly seems plausible to some people, while to the vast majority it seems utterly improbable and ridiculous. But you only have to know a little bit about Donald Trump, paedophilia, conspiracy theories and concern yourself with satanic rings to be able to construct such a version of reality.

As someone who largely grew up in an Evangelical church, I am also interested in the way labels are used not just to identify groups, but to disenfranchise other groups. An apparently simple question such as: 'Have you been born again?' is something of a tribal trope. How you answer will depend on the extent to which you feel comfortable belonging to that group, or indeed how comfortable the group feel in adopting you into their membership. Similar questions have been asked politically in the past. 'Have you ever been or are you a member of the Communist Party?' is an interesting question in north London, but rather a more disturbing question when posed during the McCarthy trials in the 1950s. Am I a liberal? Well, I guess the question depends on what you mean by 'liberal'. I like to think of myself as broadminded and curious, open to new ideas and committed to equality, and I also believe that I do not have all the answers. Does that make me a liberal? I don't think so, but a lot of people would disagree, and impute or impugn that upon me.

I think that when approaching a subject like this, it's important to remember that it's basically pretty difficult to think for yourself. By that I don't mean that you can't have an independent or original thought in your head, or that everybody else does the thinking for you. What I do mean by this is that our thinking inevitably reaches for culture, language, social constructions of reality and common experiences that already pre-shape our thinking long before we arrive at any original thought. You might think that this is particularly dangerous in a cult or a sect and is something that does not afflict the mainstream of society. But in fact, there isn't one human being who has lived in history nor one human group that's existed in history that hasn't had its thinking done for it. And it is out of that foundation that people think.

I've always loved and admired Tom Stoppard's fabulous play *Jumpers*, first performed in 1972, in which Professor George Moore debates what things might be like if they have the appearance of being one way, but in fact are not that way at all. So, what does it look like if the sun rises and rotates around the Earth? It looks very much like what we see. But suppose we imagine that what we believe – that Earth rotates around the sun – is wrong, and in fact it only looks like that (Stoppard 1972).

The apparatus for thinking that exists in our heads is largely a product of our socialisation at various life stages: from infancy to schooling to adulthood, all shaped by tribes, groups, communities and nations to which we belong. Out of such basic things come a variety of by-products both positive and negative: health and good relationships on one side, antisemitism and racism on the other, for example.

It takes rebels and dissenters to create movements to crack open the paradigms of knowledge and to shake the foundations of knowing for humanity to take a leap forward. The Renaissance is one such movement, the Reformation another: revolutions by and large of similar ilk. They change the way we think.

In the aforementioned *The Righteous Mind*, Haidt tried to understand how people disagreed with one another with such passion: not only about politics and religion, but all manner of things that to earlier and later generations would seem trivial and pointless. The genius of Haidt's work is its dependence on humanity and the very basic but perceptive insight that intuition tends to come first, and strategic reasoning comes second. This is important because moral intuitions, and I guess to some extent religious and political ones, tend to arise almost naturally and instantaneously long before moral, religious and political reasoning steps in.

This allows Haidt to say that our moral arguments are very often at best ad hoc post-constructions crafted out of more strategic objectives. The thing about these moral, political and religious reasons is that they bring groups together and they can often blind people to alternatives. All this triggers what we might term a moral matrix. For example, I hate all kinds of inequalities, but that doesn't make me a Communist. I suspect it does make me a rather poor socialist, however. I also know that inequalities are inherent within societies, groups, communities and families, and so they are unavoidable. My moral matrix must work out of my gut hostility towards inequality and my recognition that in order to persuade people towards a more equal society, I will need to develop a moral matrix of reasoning, which in itself is socially and intellectually persuasive. The irony is that that in itself, of course, requires an inequality to be developed: namely an educated elite and some practitioners who operate as leaders or exemplars.

> Thus, when the frustrated congregate in a mass movement, the air is heavy-laden with suspicion. There is prying and spying, tense watching and a tense awareness of being watched. The surprising thing is that this pathological mistrust within the ranks leads not to dissension but to strict conformity. Knowing themselves continually watched, the faithful strive to escape suspicion by adhering zealously to prescribed behaviour and opinion. Strict orthodoxy is as much the result of mutual suspicion as of ardent faith. (Hoffer 1964, pp. 124–7)

C. S. Lewis is extremely well known for his Christian writings and analogies, not least the Narnia Chronicles. But, actually, I think his views on how social formation takes place – that is, how we end up deeply inside some groups and utterly outside other groups – rank among his most interesting work. He once gave a talk that was just titled 'Membership', and although the address was given at a gathering of Christians, it has wide implications for all kinds of other groups (Lewis 1949). Lewis, of course, was able to excavate the well-trodden path between inclusion and exclusion, and also the tension between being part of a collective and being an individual. However, he thought that membership was becoming more alienating in our time: prefiguring our own time now, in which the idea of an institution for public service rather than paid-up membership has become rarer.

Robert Putnam's *Bowling Alone*, and other writers of this ilk, subscribe to the collapse in American or 'developed world' theories of soft social interactions and the subsequent effect on the production of generational values. Lewis thought that if our world lost its sense of membership, then we would become solitary and anonymous. Here is what he wrote:

> How true membership in a body differs from inclusion in a collective may be seen in the structure of a family. The grandfather, the parents, the grown-up son, the child, the dog, and the cat are true members (in the organic sense), precisely because they are not members or units of a homogeneous class. They are not interchangeable. Each person is almost a species in himself – if you subtract any one number, you've not simply reduced the family in number: you have inflicted an injury of its structure... (Putnam 2000, p. 13)

But membership can happen in various kinds of ways that are less structured and formal. Childhood books like Enid Blyton's *The Famous Five* or *The Secret Seven* give you membership of a group that doesn't depend on any kind of contract or filial obligation. What membership confers on us is shared knowledge, shared wisdom, shared experience, and shared ways of processing, which give value to the group and to the membership. As the

Bible says, the simple inherit folly, but the prudent are crowned with knowledge.

There can be a real battle between realists and relativists, non-realists and absolutists. The issue at the heart of these dialects tends to be centred on whether we can agree on what is culturally embedded. For example, if you think science is culturally embedded and the world is no longer flat, and the Earth revolves around the sun, that's almost certainly likely to condition your reading of the Psalms and social and theological constructions of reality that take place in the Old Testament, which tended to see the Earth and the cosmos in an entirely different light. The consequence of that is that you will be open to the world of metaphor, poetry and analogy, and you'll be less inclined to read Genesis as science.

> Myths are not lies. Nor are they detached stories. They are imaginative patterns, networks of powerful symbols that suggest particular ways of interpreting the world. They shape its meaning. For instance, machine imagery, which began to pervade our thought in the seventeenth century, is still potent today. We still often tend to see ourselves, and the living things around us, as pieces of clockwork: items of a kind that we ourselves could make and might decide to remake if it suits us better. Hence the confident language of 'genetic engineering' and 'the building-blocks of life'. (Midgley 2004, p. 1)

Myths are stories that are not true on the outside but are true on the inside. And funnily enough, we moderns don't think of ourselves believing in myths at all. But in fact, we are surrounded by them and shot through with them like a fish in the ocean. We drink in myths every single day with every breath we take. Our external lives envelop us in myths because they are common to all human groups, from families to churches, and from institutions to societies. This is something that Jim Hopewell was very alive to in his fascinating book *Congregation: Stories and Structures*, in which he invests considerable time and energy in decoding the storytelling and myths that govern congregational life (Hopewell 1987).

There is a famous and often-told story about the economist John Maynard Keynes, who was accused of having changed his mind on some policy issue, with the implication being that having done so, he was a bit of a flip-flopper on policy issues. Keynes is reported to have acerbically replied: 'When the facts change, Sir, I change my mind. What do you do?'

This, of course, begs the question, 'What might the facts be?' Consider this. Some years ago, I was invited to a house to perform an exorcism. If at once this sounds a little too dramatic, let me explain. Someone connected to the parish asked if the church could help with a matter that they were finding both puzzling and disturbing. A young couple with their two-year-old son had recently moved into the neighbourhood. But after some while the child had started to complain about 'seeing things' and had started to become disturbed and frightened. The boy reported seeing an elderly man wandering around the upstairs of the house, although no one else could see this. Added to which, the rooms where the appearances took place were unusually cold, despite central heating. The couple called the church, because they knew that I had worked with this sort of thing before.

What is one to make of this? I am well aware that there are potential social, psychological and psychotherapeutic angles that could be explored. However, after an interview in the home, it seemed that there were no obvious reasons for what one might call 'a lingering, disturbing and unexplained presence'. There were, for example, no deaths in the house reported by the previous occupants. Under such circumstances, I take the view that there are two priorities. First, take the presenting situation seriously as a point of pastoral need; the unexplained should not be overdramatised, or talked up as something to be feared unduly. Second, religious-type problems tend to be best addressed by religious rejoinders.

Correspondingly, I sprinkle the rooms with holy water, saying the Lord's Prayer and various Collects in all the rooms where there has been disturbance. After that, I have a cup of tea with the family, play with the child a little, and go home. Two weeks later, *en passant,* the mother mentions to me that the child slept soundly from that night, and there have been no further instances of disturbance. 'Fine,' I say, 'and thanks for the tea.'

What are we to make of this exercise in tea and empathy? As a Christian priest in a mildly liberal Anglican tradition, my answer is unequivocal: sweet nothing. The instance points us nowhere in particular. It does not confirm or deny that there are (to quote St Paul again) 'powers and principalities' to deal with that we cannot see. It does not, to me at least, prove the insuperable power of Christ over and against malign spiritual forces that govern the world unseen. So what does the encounter mean? Of course, I don't know what it means. But in my view, the encounter, and others like it that I have been part of, *points* in two contrary ways.

First, it suggests a vernacular spiritual dimension to human and social existence that needs addressing by more than mere dismissal. Second, it suggests that the grace of God, operative within imaginative *pastoralia*, elicits faith and trust, and creates a new environment of hope in which the presence of God, mediated through words and symbols, speaks and acts in fresh ways to reassure and reconfigure. Third, there is nothing to be sure of here. But there is plenty to be thankful for, including the gift of an uncertain faith that perceives it has been part of something bigger.

I realise that it is rare for theologians to speak like this, but it is important that those of us who are committed to 'faith seeking understanding' do not avoid the real spiritual questions and puzzles that absorb most people's lives. Part of the difficulty for liberal theology is that too often, it takes on the dogmatic while stressing the experiential (a legacy of the German theologian, Friedrich Schleiermacher), and yet is unwilling to scrutinise the experiential itself. Put more sharply, there are rules about frames of reference for one kind of Christian knowledge, and other rules (or is it none?) for other kinds of knowledge. As is so often the case in Christianity, fundaments find themselves exempted from appropriate critical enquiry.

Looking at life through a frame has its advantages: the picture remains in focus and frozen. The view never changes; only your view on the view alters. But for the curious, there are too many unanswered questions. Who made the frame? What lives and moves outside the frame? What aspects of the picture are obscured by the frame? It is at these junctures that an enquiring liberal mind and an accompanying spirituality start to take root. For myself, I soon realised that the frames of reference I was working with were too particular; to parody J. B. Phillips, 'your frame is too small'. The realisation that the portrait of faith I had been staring at for most of my life actually *surrounded* me, totally (but openly, not suffocatingly) changed not only my theology, but also my spirituality. Moreover, you begin to appreciate the ways in which you yourself are in the picture. The frames, suddenly, became almost redundant; they remain useful for capturing detail and focusing on issues, but their limits (as well as their relativity and selectivity) are recognised for what they are.

Spirituality makes space for surprise and excess, for the overflow of the grace of God in the hearts and minds of individuals and communities. This may sound unconvincing at first, since one does not normally associate most liberal-minded congregations with an overindulgence of worship. This is a pity, since some experiences of orthodox liberal spirituality can be intense and powerful. Moreover, because liberal piety is normally willing to adopt and adapt other modes of worship, surprises may abound in the private spiritualities of those Christians who are happy to be associated with the term 'liberal'.

For example, take the experience of speaking in tongues. I first encountered this phenomenon in my early twenties and found it both discombobulating and exhilarating to listen to. When I myself 'speak in tongues' (rare, granted), I find that it is a mildly mystical experience, and almost only ever occurs when I am alone and having a sense of deep communion with God. (Yes, I know, only an Anglican could use a phrase like 'mildly mystical experience', such are we.) I do not, by the way, consider the gift to be a 'language', but rather a kind of 'overflow' of praise, a release of the heart and mind when words will no longer do. As Danièle Hervieu-Léger puts it in her *Religion as a Chain of Memory*:

> One could ask whether the search within these communities for non-verbal forms of emotive communication does not also express a protest against the stereotyped nature of approved religious language, something about the diminished quality of articulate religious quality in modern culture. The place taken in these groups by the gift of tongues raises the questions directly ... tongues, defined by scholars as 'phonologically structured human expression without meaning, which the speaker takes to be a real language but which in fact bears no resemblance to any language living or dead,' is not a vehicle for communication but for expression. The content is of little importance: tongues finds its meanings not in what is said but in the very fact of speaking and responding, in this form, to an immediate experience of great emotional intensity. In the emotive response there is a general sensation of the presence of the divine, profound joy, and inward well-being

which finds the means of expressing itself... (Hervieu-Léger
2000, p. 59)

Tongues are certainly baffling, pothering and fothering. But for
speakers of such sounds, there is the maternal too – the sense
of being mothered by the very act of babbling, in much the
same way as an infant or toddler builds an empathetic bridge
with a parent or carer. The one uttering the sound experiences
release and joy, and it frequently radiates on their face in smiles
and expressions of sheer bliss. And, like any infant or toddler
uttering such sounds, it is not hard to imagine a smile on the
face of God by way of reciprocity, and the warm embrace that
comes. This is how we communicate, and the gift of tongues is
part of that.

5

Un-Othering Others

We begin with a matter on which all will have some opinion:
food. Specifically, its capacity to unite and divide us. 'Is there
not one bread, and one body?' asks Paul in I Corinthians 10. Yet
earlier, in I Corinthians 8, he has argued, tortuously, about the
status of meat offered to idols. Does it matter that the food we
just ate was blessed in a temple dedicated to a minor deity? His
answer is ambivalent. Yes, it might, and this could be taint by
association. But on the other hand, no, because God is God, and
idols are nothing. So eat up. But think about those with weaker
faith who will struggle with this. Also try and not let this spoil
your appetite.

To translate this into contemporary ecclesial currency, if I
objected to the ministry of women priests, or to gay clergy, can
I object only for myself and my congregation? Or can I impose
my will on the whole of my denomination, even if my views
only constitute a small minority? Why do democracy and
voting sometimes matter in the church, but sometimes don't
– and are trumped by other principles that are imposed, quite
independent of my convictions?

To return then, to the analogy of food, it would be reasonable
to go to a family restaurant and only order and eat vegetarian
food. But it would be unreasonable to complain about the other
diners in the same restaurant who were eating meat or fish.
That is their business, surely?

It is reasonable to request a vegetarian option at a steakhouse,
and no good steakhouse would be without such choices
on the menu. Yet it would be unreasonable and rude to go a
vegetarian restaurant and request a rare-cooked steak. It would
be reasonable to take over a restaurant and manage it as it was,

attracting the same custom, especially if it was the only one of its kind for miles around. But it might be less reasonable for the new manager (please note, not the owner) to refuse to offer simple food that was once on the menu because it troubled the manager's conscience. It would not be reasonable to differentiate between diners, dividing the vegetarians from the meat eaters at tables. Or to exalt those on special diets – but at the expense of most other customers.

There is something here to note about permissiveness and the liberty of conscience in any broad society. The needs and requirements of a minority, as we can see, are honoured and provided for. No one orders a steak in a vegetarian restaurant in the same way that no one ever seriously asks, 'Where is the female celebrant?' at a church where they are aware that their ministry is refused. Minority views are usually protected and can often be affirmed. But the will of this minority cannot usually be determinative for the majority.

Similarly, and with smoking, it is the case that a minority of people still like to smoke cigarettes. Smoking remains lawful, even if inadvisable. But restrictions on smoking in enclosed public spaces is legislature that came into force in the United Kingdom during 2007. Society had reached a mind – by some majority – on how the personal choices of a few might infringe the liberty of all. Smoking in public spaces was no longer a private issue – a matter for the conscience or manners of the smoker, to make a judgement on how nearby non-smokers might react. Smoking in public is deemed to be 'antisocial', and the legislation recognised that one person's liberty to smoke infringes on the well-being of others.

Discriminatory views on grounds of race, gender and disability are similar. You may think what you like in private, but you can't implement such views and practices on the public. So smokers remain free to light up in private. But they are no longer free to share (or inflict) their habit on the wider public.

Smokers effectively lost their familiar freedoms – so that wider society could gain equality of experience with fresh air in enclosed shared spaces. There was no feasible compromise.

Thus, it was not illiberal to regard 'designated smoking zones' inside restaurants as offensive and antisocial. Nor would it be 'illiberal liberalism' to resist new requests for alternative shared spaces being opened up for smokers, in order to compensate for their loss of old customary public places. We don't seek to balance the losses of privilege for smokers by yielding them some new public space. We don't say, 'Well, we banned smoking in all pubs, but as reparation, you can now smoke in certain restaurants.' Or, for that matter, set about redesignating all trains as smoking zones once again, and reintroduce specified non-smoking carriages. Nor do we suggest that smokers can light up in *your* private space, which hitherto was smoke-free.

As for passive smoking and public spaces, the claim that smokers only impact their own health has been widely refuted. In the same vein, a male bishop opposed to women priests will invariably have a widespread impact on the 'air' of the whole diocese – clergy and laity alike – quite independent of any personal or public compensatory gestures they attempt to make. That's because theological positions are inherently influential and powerful. They are conscious and subconscious; explicit and implicit. Theology affects mood and morale. Even privately held theological convictions will send unconscious coded signals that shape culture, churches and congregations: communicating acceptance or rejection, faith or doubt – just think of how classism shapes denominationalism.

What might be at stake here is trying to imagine yourself in another person's shoes, or skin, or gender. Can we? It is not easy, for sure. Is a fish conscious of the water around it, as it yearns for a larger sea or ocean? I think not. The fish has no 'experience' of the water surrounding it, until it is changed – by salt, temperature or depth. Only when such change comes does the fish experience distress. In the same way, it is hard for any of us to think and imagine outside ourselves. Few of us, if any, consciously draw and exhale each breath. Imagining otherness is something we can normally only do through meditation (for example, mindfulness attending to the breath), or when the pain we have, or the suffering of others, breaks open our frame of reference. Trauma, in other words, has its upside if you want to begin to un-other others, or be un-other-ed yourself. But this will always be, socially, a disruptive epiphany to express. The white male normativity of our world will still flinch at the otherness of colour, gender and sexuality. Like the fish in water, it takes a creative energy, curiosity and even some dissent to begin to open the frames of reference and social constructions of reality that unconsciously or consciously govern paradigms of living. Until they are called out, they remain utterly pervasive, and can be patronising, paternalistic, problematic and oppressive. Being an 'other' (or another) is costly: just ask anyone else who is.

Perhaps a better way forward is to work with boundaries, not barriers. In human spirituality the borders of faith are frequently open, because even in the most tightly compacted cult, God is a God of surprise. Even in a tribal village with a small tribal god, it is usually recognised that the deity is both outside and inside those borders. This then assumes that the only acceptable frame of reference is an open frame, which allows the viewer to look beyond the immediate and catch a glimpse of the ultimate.

A little taste of this is explored in writings such as Vincent Donovan's *Christianity Rediscovered* (Donovan 1982) and J. V. Taylor's *The Go-Between God* (Taylor 1972). Open frames of reference let God in, who is not the property of the church. Or, to paraphrase Sydney Carter (a Quaker-activist folk-hymn writer, who penned 'Lord of the Dance', amongst other songs), 'Jesus is *not* copyright of the church.' Simone Weil expresses this same dynamic better than most theologians:

For it seemed to me certain, and I still think so today, that one can never wrestle enough with God if one does so out of pure regard for the truth. Christ likes us to prefer truth to him because, before being Christ, he is truth. If one turns aside from him to go toward truth, one will not go far before falling into his arms. (Weil and Perrin 2000)

This very slight theological turn takes us towards the potential engagement with 'otherness'. Many writers have testified to its embrace of paradox. Open frames of reference are themselves a clue to the shape of liberal piety. As Alec Vidler noted:

The liberal vocation, faithfully exercised, is not only humbling but also reconciling. It has the effect of showing that no party or school of thought or phase of orthodoxy is ever as right as its protagonists are inclined to suppose and that men, including Christian [men], have much more in common both of frailty and strength, both of falsehood and truth, than the makers of systems and sects acknowledge ... A liberal-minded man is free from narrow prejudice, generous in his judgement of others, open-minded, especially in the reception of new ideas or proposals for reform. Liberal is the opposite not of conservative, but of fanatical, bigoted, or intransigent. It points to the *'esprit large'* and away from the *'idée fixe'*. (Vidler 1957, p. 32)

Vidler's words are a partial answer to those who say that liberalism worships at the altar of unknown principles and values. Actually, liberal Christianity does no such thing. But it does recognise that an imperialistic or patronising approach to the different faiths and beliefs of others is not a real part of the liberal spirit. That is not because liberals believe that all beliefs are equal. They are not. We have reasons for renouncing racism, sexism and antisemitism. Liberalism is discriminating, but it is also characterised by a generosity founded on the incomprehensible capaciousness of God, so is pre-programmed to be open to otherness (especially those who are oppressed and denied normativity).

As such, because liberalism is rooted in awe and humility, the humble spirit does not lead to relativity, but rather to deep respect of the other, and their inherent equality and value before God. So it can perhaps afford at once to be both confident yet circumspect, definable yet open, certain yet tinged with faithful doubt. In other words, it takes us to a place where we might more readily acknowledge the oft-quoted words from *The Cloud of Unknowing*: 'By love God may be gotten and holden, but by thought and understanding, never.'

As we discussed earlier, just as tongues and the maternal face of God help us to think through the ordinary nature of empathetic, joyful, loving and compassionate communication with a babbling toddler, so we can perhaps now note another enigma. One of the very earliest credal statements in the New Testament is in 2 Corinthians 4: 6 – 'For God, who said, "Let light shine out of darkness", has shone in our hearts to give the light of the knowledge of the glory of God in the face of Jesus Christ...'

It is a singularly compelling image with an infinitude of meaning. The face of God known in a human face. Our faces register pain, puzzlement and pleasure. They smile, frown and weep. They often cannot lie in the ways that our lips can sometimes do. Our faces are how we are known: on a driving licence, ID, or in a passport. And here, in 2 Corinthians 4: 6, we are told that the ultimate 'other' – God – is known in the familiarity of a *human* face. One that can be recognised, related to, remembered, slapped, struck, spat into, rejected ... And that only when we can learn to see the face of God in the faces of 'others' will we have taken one small step in the journey of un-othering others. We will see the face of God in the alien, stranger, poor, naked, hungry, homeless, prisoner – irrespective of creed, colour, gender, age, class, and more besides (Matthew 25: 44). God is indeed present in the 'other'.

If you don't believe me, here is an exercise to aim for the next time you go out on a regular shopping trip. Try looking at the people you are with, or all the people you don't know or have never ever met, and may never ever do so, *differently*. Do so with as much compassion as you can possibly muster, and with the least amount of prejudice you can get by with. Now, what do you *see*? And at this very same time, picture God raising that proverbial eyebrow, casting a measureless beaming smile across space and time, just at you, and right now. You may just get to hear God chuckling audibly in this small corner of our cavernous galaxy, across the universe: 'Hah... see, told you I was there already...'

6

Other-Wise

All civilisations have their time and season. They age and wither; they are born again; they can renew; and they can perish and be scattered as though dust in a crisp summer breeze. There is a time for everything.

> For everything there is a season,
> and a time for every matter under heaven:
>
> a time to be born, and a time to die;
> a time to plant, and a time to pluck up what is planted;
>
> a time to kill, and a time to heal;
> a time to break down, and a time to build up;
>
> a time to weep, and a time to laugh;
> a time to mourn, and a time to dance;
>
> a time to cast away stones, and a time to gather stones together;
> a time to embrace, and a time to refrain from embracing;
>
> a time to seek, and a time to lose;
> a time to keep, and a time to cast away;
>
> a time to tear, and a time to sew;
> a time to keep silence, and a time to speak;
>
> a time to love, and a time to hate;
> a time for war, and a time for peace.

The scriptures – in all faiths – are full of wisdom, pregnant with and gestating the great existential questions that are set before us for all time. Into that space the Spirit of God continually searches for and sifts us, calling us to become the persons and peoples that can make God's difference to the lives of others. Our fulfilment lies in connecting with those others, and our vocation is in serving, supporting and enabling them as our equals. When we relieve the poor of suffering, the broken-hearted of their grief, and the condemned of their shame, we sing of God.

During this recent global pandemic, I have found myself watching quite a number of films that revolve around the rise and fall of empires. I have watched a wide range of documentaries on democracy and the birth of new political movements. I always enjoy stories of justice, dissent and moral courage. The documentaries and dramas that usually have the biggest impact on me are ones concerned with toppling.

Now, here you might think of the statue of Edward Colston (1636–1721), who made his money from slave trading, being tipped into the harbour in Bristol at the hands of those protesting about continued racism in their city and society. Or perhaps the much discussed (but frankly, not very obvious) small statue of Cecil Rhodes (1853–1902) in Oriel Square, Oxford. I think of Saddam Hussein (1937–2006) and his statue. I think of almost any days spent in the British Museum, and any part of it, and the statues to people who were, of their time, worth carving in stone.

As we all die, so are nearly all statues destined to be toppled. 'Toppling' is one of the most ambiguous words in the English language. It can mean to 'put a top on' and to 'cut the top off' and 'shave the head'. Charles I was toppled in all senses and is one of the few monarchs to have been beheaded (1649), yet also to make it into the Anglican Calendar of Saints (Charles, King and Martyr – Feast Day 30 January). Perhaps he'd rather have kept his head. But I am not sure. He had a martyr complex, of that, I am sure. To topple is 'to finish' (including a bad ending), but also to 'fill up, add more to bring to fullness'. It can mean to 'tumble down, to fall headfirst' and to 'be tipped over'. It is therefore even more remarkable that 'tip-toe' only has one meaning.

Our beliefs, and the beliefs of others, are invariably founded on topplings. Wisdom will always confound us, and so to engage with wisdom is to lose ourselves and our presumptions and assumptions, only to be found again, and reconstituted. Wisdom is knowing our place before God. It is from that place that we can regard others – all others – as made in God's image and equal with us in God's sight. There is nothing and no one for which God does not have regard. In an influential essay by Dan Hardy, he writes that

> The task of theology, then, is to begin from common practice and examine its quality in open trial by the use of natural reason in order to discover the truth of this practice, by a truth-directed reason ... (including) practical reason. And the outcome ... should be an agreement on the proper organisation of common life which would actually promote the practice of society ... The concern is public ... the use of public reason, open trial of the truth and the achievement of truly social existence. (Hardy 1989, p. 33)

I find this to be a rather compelling vision for theology: public, corporate, listening, attentive, forward-looking, open to 'natural reason' and committed to the discovery of truth. I wonder if such a theological vision might also be a social vision, at the same time, for how we regard others? Might we be willing, with our beliefs, to see them subjected to that 'open trial of truth' that Hardy speaks of? The 'achievement of a truly social existence' might be something our politicians, church leaders and social campaigners could bring about, if lived in light and truth.

Wisdom, as the psalmist confirms, is 'knowing your place before God'. Such knowledge leads us to humility, unless you happen to be a delusional narcissist. For we are asked to model ourselves on the one who humbled himself, and 'became obedient unto death', as Philippians 2 goes on to say. Christ emptied himself and became a servant. His love is a kenotic affair: a self-emptying sacrifice. God un-others God-self, and in so doing becomes one of us, so we might be one with God, and one with another. Only un-othering ourselves can help us appreciate, give thanks for, and love the other.

Humility is the quality of being humble. But in our person-centred, fulfilment-therapeutically-attuned culture, we often conflate humility with humiliation. We assume low self-regard and unworthiness to be debasing. But in religion, humility is rooted in perspective and submission – and being 'un-selved', a liberation from consciousness of the self; a form of *temperance* that is neither having pride (or haughtiness) nor indulging in self-deprecation.

True humility comes, ironically, from a deep inner self-confidence, and attends to the needs of and the valuing of others. The humble person is not preoccupied with themselves but, rather, occupied with the needs of others. Humiliation, in contrast, is imposed on us externally, and this frequently shames us.

Now, you might think that humility is unattainable, and humiliation undesirable. But both terms are linked to the words 'humus' and 'hubris'. 'Humus' means being earthed, and the humble person is ultimately a grounded person: sure of their being, so not above themselves – and knows they are not better than any others, no matter what giftedness, rank or status they hold. 'Hubris', in contrast, is self-inflated, puffed-up self-perception, and it lacks groundedness.

Humanity and spirituality are an endless series of tutorials in the understanding and practice of love. Becoming a person is a life-long course of tutorials, tests and assignments, you will already know that your own thinking and performance in this applied dramaturgy is extremely difficult to award marks for. Indeed, you are under constant evaluation, and there is no final exam. Life and love are matters of continuous assessment, albeit a difficult one to grade.

So if you wish to understand and excel at humanity, think of others, and of humility; think of love – and only then yourself – as being something that is *earthed* in doing normal, simple, mundane things for others. Love is rooted in humility: stopping to care for the small details and concerns of other people's lives *matters*.

I have often had course to reflect on what matters. Wherever I go, I carry in my pocket one tangible sign of this: a hazelnut. It has only purpose: to reinforce that God cares for the tiniest nut, and not just me. Or you. Or others. It is a reminder of those words from Julian of Norwich. She wrote:

And in this he showed me a little thing, the quantity of a hazelnut, lying in the palm of my hand. It was as round as any ball.

I looked upon it with the eye of my understanding, and thought,

'What may this be?' And it was answered generally thus, 'It is all that is made.'

I marvelled how it might last, for I thought it might suddenly have fallen to nothing for littleness.

And I was answered in my understanding: It lasts and ever shall, for God loves it.

And so have all things their beginning by the love of God. In this little thing I saw three properties.

The first that God made it. The second that God loves it.

The third, that God keeps it...

In the days ahead, as we face many challenges in our country, communities and wider world, hold fast to God and no less to one another. God will keep us, and keep other-ed. Stay grounded. Be humble. God is faithful. Perhaps this is the beginning of becoming other-wise – having a wisdom about others, and ourselves.

I decided to write this short book during a time of global pandemic, and numerous national crises and emergencies. Old orders are being toppled as I write, and it is possible that new forms of polity and sociality are being born. For many people this has been a time of personal crisis. In our country, more than 150,000 have died of the effects of Covid-19 – more than the number lost in the Blitz of the Second World War. One cannot fathom the disruption and destruction that the virus continues to wreak.

It has been a time of personal crisis for me too. I have found myself 'other-ed' as a deviant, and been subjected to foul and abusive denigration, demonisation and marginalisation. In this, I have begun to glimpse the world of Kafka and Orwell, and begin to have some inkling of what it must have been like to live as John Proctor in Arthur Miller's play *The Crucible* (1953). Frankly, if enough people say that you are a Communist, heretic, spy, political deviant, a risk because you are classed as insane or some other threat, a leper, or perhaps a pariah... well then, you are. Just as our communities once other-ed women and burned them as witches, so in our own society, even in its most (seemingly) civilised quarters, small ghettoes can spring up as forms of self-protection for vulnerable minorities.

In our world, we can easily see intelligent people allowing themselves to become consumed by the dysfunctional kinds of groupthink that the psychologist and relational theorist Wilfred Bion wrote so compellingly of. It takes courage to speak out against wilful prejudice that can feel like a form of emotional and reasoned coercion. Black Lives Matter is a witness to what must sometimes be done to speak against the blinkered narcolepsy and privilege of white normativity. Sometimes the only way to level the playing field is to topple the statues.

This book has not got a lot to say about God, but it has been about issuing a gentle invitation to regard others quite differently. As equally and wonderfully made as you are. Wisdom is knowing your place before God (Psalm 139; and see Proverbs 9: 10). So, as Christ did so fully and completely, do what you can to be open, and occupy yourself with God; and let God occupy you with the cares and concerns that God, Christ and the Spirit have for our broken world.

Put others before yourself. Clothe yourself in humility. God gives grace to the humble. Like Atlas, hold up the skies and those around you, and don't expect to be thanked for it, or even perhaps acknowledged. You probably won't be. But humble yourself, and you will be exalted.

Like the story of Jonah (surely one of the most powerful short stories that we have – but incomplete), the gospels leave us with the possibility of a sequel; with loose ends not tied up. Consider the Gospel of Mark, who ends his narrative with these words – *ephobounto gar* – 'for they were afraid'. What kind of conclusion is that? The resurrection has apparently just happened, and the salvation of the world set in motion – but 'they were afraid' does not inspire confidence. The ending points to something more *to come.*

As the pastoral theologian and essayist Eugene Peterson points out (Peterson 1992), this word *gar* (for) is a transitional one; *The sentence leaves* you ready for whatever the next part of the *story* is – except there isn't *yet* one *in the story*. There is just a blank space, a pause. Mark's Gospel *seems to* finish mid-*thought*, I think, deliberately, *leaving* us off-balance, mid-stride: where will the next step be? This is artful reticence; a conclusion is *withheld* from the disciples and the reader. It is now up to you to say what happens next, and then act. In other words, the Christian faith cannot be wrapped up as a finished product. The frame is open; the picture not yet complete. As Peterson says, 'write a resurrection conclusion with your own life.' Become other-wise.

7

The Others Next Door
(Neighbourhood Watch)

In Joel Robbins' fine *Becoming Sinners: Christianity and Moral Torment in a Papua New Guinea Society* (Robbins 2004), we encounter the Urapmin – a remote people never directly 'missionised'. Dwelling amidst one of the numerous impassable valleys, packed with dense jungle, they were reached by Baptist missionaries in the early 1960s. Or, rather, they reached the missionaries – for the Urapmin began in the 1960s to send young men to study with Baptist missionaries living among the neighbouring communities.

In a world of swift and sweeping cultural transformations, few have seen changes as rapid and dramatic as those experienced by the Urapmin of Papua New Guinea. By the late 1970s, the Urapmin had undergone a charismatic revival, abandoning their traditional religion for a Christianity intensely focused on human sinfulness and driven by a constant sense of millennial expectation. Robbins' shrewd and careful ethnography gives us compelling insights into the Urapmin. They have no word in their language for the colour we know as 'blue', since all above them is a high canopy of bright green forest. The highest trees and the sky are as one in this construction of reality. When a member of the Urapmin suffers from a common cold, they believe that with every sneeze discharging nasal mucus (commonly known as snot), this is part of your brain that is lost. I guess if you have a very heavy cold, that is exactly what it can feel like.

Robbins' book explores how the Urapmin, in order to become Christians, first of all have to other themselves and become sinners. Their sins, naturally, are related to their means of living. One of the worst sins is to overly admire or envy your neighbours' harvest. Or their lunch or family meal. To be saved, the Urapmin must first do something quite alien to their society: they need to re-narrate themselves as lost. Joel Robbins shows how their preoccupations provided keys to understanding the nature of cultural change more generally. Their millennial expectations are regular and frequent. Indeed, the imminent return of Christ is anticipated several times over the course of a few years. This leads the Urapmin to down tools, move into the mission hut, fast, and pray, and wait. Eventually they will emerge (often after a prophecy bids them return to work, and to prepare harder next time). And so life continues, with the rhythm of revival interwoven with the harvests and the times and seasons, such as·they are.

In one sense, living with the Urapmin might be much like living in any village, anywhere in the world. In *My Sweet Little Village* (Menzel 1985), a Czech film comedy from 1985, before the Berlin Wall came down (1989), we are introduced to a handful of folk in a ramshackle village some hours from Prague. The film is beautifully poised. For years the overbearing Pavek has endured Otik, who is disabled, sharing his meals and the front seat of their truck. But Otik is such a sweet-natured chump that Pavek, exasperated as he becomes, never follows through with his warnings that he will go and find another partner. I have long admired the film for the touching way in which it affirms local knowledge (always better than what town and city folk think is best); resilience (keeping the townies and city folk out of their lives, and ensuring outsiders never get to purchase any local property); fortitude (the economy in the village is richer with less, and the apparent wealth of the town and city folk are not much cared for); morality (high thresholds of toleration for indiscretions, which can usually be resolved over a few beers, and the odd fist fight if absolutely necessary – no one ever really gets hurt); medicine and mortality (the local doctor and nurse are best described as 'pragmatic', and have a rather winsome attitude to life and death – some illnesses are not worth the trouble: you are going to die anyway); and finally Communism, commerce, government and civic order (all suitably subverted by local knowledge at every juncture – so much so, you wonder why Stalin ever bothered).

If you have ever lived in a village yourself, you will recognise Robbins' world or Menzel's tiny Czech community. Having lived in a rural English village for ten years, I can testify to the power of local knowledge, and the extraordinary way in which its proponents regard it as superior to most other kinds of knowing. In the village I lived in, a local farmer tapped into the electricity grid every year to light up the Christmas tree on the village green. The village had not paid any electricity bill for their street lights (they had twelve) since the early 1950s. They all kept quiet about that. The village had a Neighbourhood Watch scheme, the primary task of which, so far as I could see, was to file reports of visiting 'strangers' (any kind) with the local police. A stranger was defined by one villager as 'someone we don't know, and so we don't know who they are, or what their business is, or what they're up to'. There was no chance of small acts of petty crime or, for that matter, illicit liaisons being kept secret. They knew who thieved, and they knew who was seeing who, and on what terms. Everyone knew everyone else's business.

I loved living there and marvelled at how certain feuds between neighbours were passed down through family lineage, long after the original focal points of dispute had any further point. Chairing their local parish council required a dexterity normally reserved for top mediators, the United Nations Council, marital counselling, family therapy and the Northern Ireland peace accord. Sometimes a single council meeting could generate all these dynamics. And yet the village and its identity was a triumph of neighbourliness, charity and care. As an institution, the village had something approaching the kind of 'total' life that one might observe in a much more obvious form of organisation (for example, church, club, union, etc.). Here, there are various ways of regarding others. Do we pay attention to their symbols, codes of behaviour, patterns of believing and belonging, or other aspects that might account for why a group self-identifies as 'we' and 'us' – but not 'them'?

The symbolic anthropology of David Schneider (1918–95) argued that systems of society should not be separated into bits and linked to particular aspects of social organisation – for example, economy and politics, or categories like kinship and religion – but rather studied as wholes. Interpretive anthropology, which began with Edward Evans-Pritchard's work on Azande witchcraft and Nuer religion, has come to be most associated with the work of the American anthropologist Clifford Geertz (1926–2011). Geertz proposed the study of cultural systems as texts, or acted documents, to be studied by building up the details of cultural life as thick description, a methodology of doing ethnography. Geertz criticised what he called Levi-Strauss's 'cerebral savages' and his 'cryptological' approach, which analysed symbols as closed structures rather than texts built out of social materials. In his 1966 article 'Religion as a Cultural System', Geertz defined religion as a system of symbols, which acts to establish powerful, pervasive and long-lasting moods and motivations in folk by formulating conceptions of a general order of existence and clothing these conceptions with such an aura of factuality that the moods and motivations seem uniquely realistic (Geertz and Darnton 2017).

The mention of 'moods' here is interesting. It reminds us of a question once posed by John Caputo, the theologian-philosopher: how do churches, church leaders and congregations 'convey the mood of God'? In some respects, ecclesial differences are all about understanding why the apparent 'mood of God' has been reified and expressed in different churches. Some moods are light, others heavy. Some warm, others decidedly cool, or even cold. Some passionate, others cerebral. Of course, anthropologists cannot tell us what God's 'mood' is, only that churches will often reflect what they think God's mood is. A mood is the motional condition and frame of mind of an individual or body. It is the 'inner weather' of a culture, perhaps?

In the early part of the twentieth century, anthropology was typically concerned with small-scale, technologically simple societies. In part this was out of a desire to record ways of life that were rapidly changing with the advent of colonialism (although it would be a mistake to assume that these societies were somehow unchanging, or even truly isolated, before their contact with the West) and in part it was out of a desire to get at the 'essential' or 'elementary' forms of human institutions (although it would also be a mistake to assume that matters such as law or religion are somehow more 'basic' in these societies).

Dialogue is the backbone of ethnography. While anthropologists make use of a variety of techniques to elicit and record data, the interview is by far the most important. Interviews can range in formality from highly structured question-and-answer sessions, to the recording of life histories, to informal conversations, or to a chance exchange during an unanticipated encounter. Ultimately, the key to ethnographic success is *being there*. When patterns of behaviour and ideology become relatively discrete, enduring and autonomous, we call these patterns 'institutions'. The most extreme form of institutions of these are those that Erving Goffman – one of the foremost American sociologists and social psychologists – called the 'total institutions': the military, prisons, boarding schools, communes, cults, psychiatric hospitals, and so on. These are organisations that govern virtually all facets of their members' lives. Individuals are typically stripped of previous social identities: their heads may be shaved; their clothes are replaced with uniforms; they lose access to many of their personal possessions; their everyday behaviour is strictly regulated; and they are subject to the absolute authority of their immediate superiors. A church or theological college can be a kind of 'total institution'.

If you study religious cults and new religious movements, as I have done, you quickly realise that it is in this highly suggestive state that followers learn the institution's unique way of doing, thinking and feeling that may not necessarily be shared by the society at large. They are drawn into the 'discipline' of the 'bounded life', in other words. This experience is transformative, and years after leaving such an institution it can continue to play a profound role in the individual's thoughts and feelings. The extreme degree of control and rigid patterning of behaviour total institutions create can often produce morally extreme results, from monastics living a life of holiness to the suffering inflicted upon the inmates of a concentration camp.

You may well be thinking to yourself, 'But I have no experience of such things.' If so, think again. Mary Midgley's excellent study – *Wickedness* (1984) – borrows from one of Erich Fromm's works on concentration camps (*The Anatomy of Human Destructiveness*, 1973) in which he points out that one of the common human fallacies is that we cannot believe in destructive and malicious humanity – even evil Nazis – and so assume that everybody who commits evil is some kind of demon or devil. No one will take responsibility for the sin of Cain against Abel – it is as though such conduct was a freak occurrence of human nature.

We lose sight of the fact that many evil people can be kind, and most certainly charming. They have a sense of humour, and are often married, with children. A belief in devils, demons and hell transfers human nature and ordinary social conduct into a spiritual realm. When we do this, we find we are constantly at the mercy of being duped by evil intentions and acts, and are therefore shocked, dismayed – and disbelieving and angry

– when we find such conduct under our noses. Institutions of all kinds provide ample camouflage, escapes, hiding places and open platforms for evil. Faced with determined wickedness, kindness is limited in what it can achieve.

Now you may think that if you have no experience of a total institution, although it is likely you went to school, where there would have been some regulation of clothing – even if no official uniform. Typically, dress codes will correspond to certain requirements: practical, conformist and classless will often be important. However, many will be modest too. Mention of modesty may seem innocuous, but all cultures, anywhere, have some concept that conforms to our notions of 'modesty'. Within any given culture it will be applied differently to men and women, children and adults, and differently to the powerful and the less powerful. Typically, a given culture will regard its own standards of modesty as 'natural' rather than being culturally relative or socially determined. This is, of course, not the case, as any plain reading of the history of fashion will yield.

That said, in every age and in every culture, modesty will have acquired *moral* value, such that a given culture may regard others with stricter standards as prudes, and those with laxer standards as loose. Modesty finds its way from clothing into television, film, literature and other media. Cultures will have ideas of what is seemly and unseemly, rude, amusing, banal and blasphemous. The content of what fits within these cultural silos will vary widely and arbitrarily across time and space. Indeed, what will be regarded as thoroughly immodest in one place at one time will be regarded as quite proper elsewhere at another time.

So, to us, our neighbours may seem slack or uptight, liberal or conservative, prudish or loose, progressive or traditional. These silos in themselves will be filled with different patterns of behaviour, beliefs, social attitudes and outlooks, and morals. Our neighbours are often othered by us because all societies have interests in what we might term the 'regulation of passions' – which can include our responses to films (for example, nudity, horror, sex, etc.), television and other media often carrying recommended age-related (or restricted) regulation.

Likewise, ages of consent vary from culture to culture, and also their rationale. For example, we might construe the mid-teens as a reasonable age for agreeing on a concept of sexual 'consent'. But this means a sixteen-year-old in a full sexual relationship with a fifteen-year-old might still be illegal. Other societies prefer to look at the age gap between the parties. Here, sex between fifteen- and fourteen-year-olds may not be so problematic, but between a sixteen-year-old and a twenty-five-year-old might be regarded as potentially abusive. Similarly, deciding on rights and the law is often rooted in cultural judgements about modesty, which will explain the eternal cycle of a parent trying to chide their daughter thus: 'You are not going out dressed in that! And that top needs to be at least two inches higher, and your skirt three inches longer... Now, go upstairs and get changed... now!' etc.

What must be borne in mind is that 'we' and 'us' are not 'them', and our propensity for othering – even our next-door neighbour – is part of how we construct our social world, and so is part of our theo-socio-moral construction of reality. I only have to think of one of my neighbours in the village I used to live in and remember how they used to describe the people down the hill – less than quarter of a mile away, but a place that, he would assure me, was well below par and unworthy of respectable folk like himself. After a few pints in the pub, he could be ruder still, but would then usually also let slip that he himself had been born at the bottom of that same hill. His apparent hard-and-fast boundaries (*extremely* 'local') were, in fact, a cluster of contradictions, judgements and ambivalences. As for his beliefs, well, they were there. Likewise, his certainties and own local knowledge reigned supreme. Provided you remembered that, and were prepared to dismiss any contradicting facts or expertise you might be harbouring, he was, nonetheless, a good neighbour.

8

Suggested Questions and Exercises
for Groups

This very short book was designed as a modest stimulant for thinking. It is intended for groups that like to study (perhaps the Bible, or a book club, or a gathering that explores spirituality, faith, etc.). It will be obvious as you read it through that it raises more questions than it answers. It does not attempt to do anything other than this.

There are some light exercises you can try to limber up in a discussion. I recommend reading some of the short 'Ladybirds for Grown-Ups', with titles such as *The Ladybird Book of the People Next Door* (2016) or *The Story of Brexit* (2018) – both books written by Jason Hazeley and Joel Morris. They are achingly funny (if you are of a certain persuasion), and quite hard work if you are not. However, because the books are effectively conduits for venting suspicion, bias and even contempt, the reader, even if sympathetic to the bias of the books, will invariably be pressed into some self-critical reflection on their own prejudices.

If your group is interested in thinking through some of the more pressing contemporary political and social issues, I commend Denise Cottrell-Boyce's *Welcoming the Stranger* (Darton, Longman & Todd 2021). This is one of the books from the publisher in their 'How the Bible Can Help Us Understand' series. The books use novels, personal stories, suggestions for individual and group reflections, and of course, portions of scripture. The books take a more angular look at issues, and are likely to appeal to groups that foster exploration and welcome curiosity. You might also try engaging with a non-religious text at the same time, and I warmly commend Malcolm Gladwell's *Talking to Strangers* (Penguin 2020), billed in the subtitle as 'what we should know about the people we don't know'.

You might also give some thought to reading around the topic of listening. What does it mean to really tune in to another person's life? How can we enter into the experience of others? On one level, we can't. But the foundations for empathy, deep sympathy and, ultimately, compassion lie somewhere within our ability to enter into the lives of others. Kathryn Mannix's *Listen: How to Find the Words for Tender Conversations* (Collins 2021) is a good introduction for individuals and groups. Why do we avoid difficult conversations? Why do we tend to skirt around what matters most? Mannix sees tenderness and kindness as being key to listening. We cannot speak our hearts and minds (though we love to do so!) until we have learned to sound the depths of and truly hear others.

We cannot understand others unless we listen. Deep listening comes before deep literacy – the capacity to comprehend others. We begin with tenderness, humility and kindness, so that we constantly recognise there is always 'someone other than me' to be accommodated. If we don't make space for them in our conversations, deliberations and society, there will always be too many people feeling that they are never heard. Women who have campaigned – loudly and longingly – for equality (e.g., suffrage, equality in the workplace, ordination, against sexism, etc.) are instructive. Shouting is a response to indifference and deliberate deafness.

Those who are snubbed, patronised, oppressed or marginalised because of their sexuality, ethnicity or class will also raise their voices in pain and protest. Tender listening is not just a form of pastoral care. Done properly, with integrity, it is one of the first stages in political action. After all, if you are not going to be changed yourself as a result of listening to the pain and alienation of others, and work to change their world, why would you bother giving them the time of day in the first place? When you listen, ask yourself, 'Now, what am I going to do for this person or this group, as a result of hearing them and their pain?'

Those in pain and toiling under the heel of oppression seldom lack for sympathy or empathy. What they seek is something else, namely your support for change: your agency. So, when you next listen to someone, ask yourself if you are really prepared to *hear* that person, and work to change their world. Listening is a political act, as much as speaking is. What the world needs now, more than ever, is emotionally intelligent, kind-hearted and tender conversations that are fearless in care.

Book clubs that would prefer to work with other non-religious texts could begin with taking a chapter a week from Jessica Nordell's *The End of Bias: How We Change Our Minds* (Granta Publications 2021) or Jennifer L. Eberhardt's *Biased: Uncovering the Hidden Prejudices That Shape Our Lives* (Random House 2019). Both authors explore unintentional bias and the persistent prejudices that often clash with our more consciously held beliefs. Nordell writes with warmth and humour, and is prepared to take on subjects such as the prevalence of diversity training courses in organisations, and why they often fall short.

Christian groups wanting to get to grips with bias might begin with Robert P. Jones' work on systemic racism in mainstream denominations in the USA. His *White Too Long: The Legacy of White Supremacy in American Christianity* (Simon & Schuster 2020) and *The End of White Christian America* (Simon & Schuster 2017) provide excellent materials for reflection and discussion that will work well for groups, and his writing and analysis is superbly researched. If you are embarking on group work with the books I have suggested, or others, do make sure that those participating are willing to listen and speak respectfully, and also able to cope with disagreements and divisions that cannot be resolved. Having a different opinion and belief from your neighbour is quite normal. The ethical question that arises is, therefore, 'How do we live together despite our differences?'

To that end, readers and groups may want to look in more depth at the work of Jonathan Haidt, whose work is briefly touched on in this book. Haidt is an exponent of moral foundations theory, and so has a keen interest in bias, and how we speak of and treat 'others', and how we, as others, are in turn spoken of and treated. There are always journeys to make, bridges to cross, and fences to mend. According to moral foundations theory, the differences in people's moral concerns can be described in terms of five spectrums of moral foundations:

1 *Care* or *harm*: cherishing and protecting others; the opposite of *uncaring* and *injury*.
2 *Fairness* or *proportionality*: rendering justice with shared rules; the opposite of *cheating*.
3 *Loyalty* or *betrayal*: *in-group*: standing with your group, family, nation; the opposite of *allegiance* or *infidelity*.
4 *Authority* or *respect*: submitting to tradition/legitimate authority; the opposite of *subversion*.
5 *Sanctity* or *purity*: abhorrence/disgust of things, foods, actions; the opposite of *degradation*.

These five foundations fit within a framework of two higher-order clusters –
a. the person-focused *individualising* cluster of care and fairness
b. the group-focused *binding* cluster of loyalty, authority and sanctity.

A sixth foundation, *liberty* (the opposite of *oppression*) was theorised by Jonathan Haidt in his *The Righteous Mind* (2012). Researchers found that people's sensitivities to the five/six moral foundations correlate with their political ideologies. Liberals are most sensitive to the care and fairness axis. Conservatives tend to favour loyalty, authority and sanctity dimensions. According to Haidt, the differences have significant implications for our political discourse and relations. Because members of specific political camps are, to a degree, blind to one or more of the favoured moral foundations of the others, they may perceive any morally driven words or behaviour as having another basis entirely – at best self-interested, and at worst evil, and thus will then demonise the 'other'.

It is likely that liberals will orientate towards the care/fairness/ individual-justice pole. Opposition to this position – which is group-orientated, and will be group/church/party members – will emphasise group/tribe/family loyalty (so don't betray); respect for authority (whether right or not, so no subversion allowed); the sanctity of the tribe/group (so questioning this may cause its degradation). Care of individuals will invariably be sacrificed to avoid potential proportional harm that may be caused to the group.

The cost of questioning behaviours/practices among the group/tribe is high: one is likely to be stigmatised as deviant, eccentric or worse. Only external intervention penetrating the tribe, such as justice/law, or a case of disproportionate excessive harm (for example, suicide of a colleague) brings behaviours and actions to an end. Even then (for example, the murderer of Jo Cox MP), alienating/socially damaging tribal rhetoric may nonetheless continue to justify/accommodate evil.

Most good education, decent theology, quite a lot of spirituality, and certainly nearly all faith development, is conversational in character. We learn as we listen, and we are often changed when we truly hear. We also listen when we speak, as when we come to put words to our experiences, we discover their partiality and paucity – but also authenticity. Things we valued and thought we were absolutely sure of don't quite attain the currency we supposed they were worth when we speak of them. So we listen in a spirit of humility, even to ourselves. On the other hand, some things that might have seemed worthless to us are, to others, surprising nuggets of gold, and cherished as treasure.

If you are minded to use this short book as a basis for discussion, I recommend that you set some ground rules for listening and speaking with one another. It is far too easy in group dynamics to fall into unhelpful binaries, like listener-speaker and leader-led. I take a different approach, and suggest you try to inhabit the beliefs and worldview of others from the outset.

For example, you might like to have a discussion about how your beliefs and values on sexuality and religion have changed – or stayed the same – over the course of your life. Have you always thought what you now think? Were there any experiences, meetings or people from the past that began to change or intensify the way you believed? When did you last hear a sermon on this subject, and how did it make you feel, and what did it make you think?

Then, rather than tell the group all of this, spend no more than five minutes summarising this to the person sitting nearest you. They may not interrupt you in these five minutes. Your partner may make notes, and they may ask questions for clarification for no more than two minutes at the end. Then reverse roles. Having both made notes, and the rest of the group likewise, your partner then speaks for you for around three minutes, summarising what they (hopefully!) have heard. Their introduction of you should be positive, fair and not subjected to the interspersing of any qualifying comments or criticism, as though reading a text. The presentation of your beliefs and experiences should be undertaken by your partner *at least* as an advocate or attorney might for a defendant in a case. Ideally, however, they would speak not just for you, but as you – in role, occupying and owning your beliefs and values, and done as though this is all that matters. All in the group should do likewise for the other, as an act of generous hospitality.

Having listened to one another, one person can take responsibility for moderating a discussion, and drawing the common threads together. But the group should also carefully note the areas that have seemed peripheral, and which perhaps only one person mentioned or touched on. The group can then reflect, later, on how discussion of these experiences and beliefs might be taken forward.

This can be a difficult process, to be sure. But trust it and stay with it, and each other. It can be hard for the person who has major misgivings about same-sex marriages to spend some time living in the experience and beliefs who will embody and represent those very misgivings. But we cannot understand others unless we take these kinds of steps.

Proceeding in this way will enable the group to develop respectful, empathetic and possibly compassionate modes of listening, which can otherwise be lost if we find ourselves pressed in self-defence over our beliefs and values. Listening and speaking like this can help us begin to own what it is like to be the 'other person' – someone else – with their life, beliefs and experiences, and the pleasure and rewards that these may bring, or perhaps the pain and stigma that they might also impugn. Some beliefs are a liberating gift; others can be an oppressing burden. Remember, most people who hold sincere beliefs don't think they chose them, as though on a shopping spree. Many people harbour a view that these beliefs chose them. They don't hold beliefs; they are held *by* them.

Each portion of this short book would make for a reasonable discussion of around ninety minutes or so, and as there are seven segments, there will be enough material for a Lent group, or to keep you busy for a couple of months, or another season, say between Easter and Trinity Sunday. Or for students, for a term, or half a semester. It would be tendentious to produce a lengthy list of questions at this point, but let me offer you a few ideas to help get you started.

1. Some of our beliefs were (literally) infantile (for example, the tooth fairy). What was it like to lose those beliefs? How should we respond to adults whom we might imagine still hold infantile beliefs?
2. Beliefs live side by side with values. What did you grow up with, and how did you come to be a moral, spiritual being?
3. Are there any aspects of your faith tradition that you sit light with, or prefer not to believe at all? How do you relate to people in your faith tradition that strongly hold on to and stand by these beliefs?
4. Sometimes the experiences and encounters we have can confound us, and we find we are radically changed. Can you describe a moment or season that has changed the way you think, believe and live?
5. The thing about other people is that we never really understand how they tick until we get to know them better. How has a relationship with someone 'other' altered the way you see them, and yourself?
6. Wisdom often surfaces when we least expect it, and from sources that we would not normally have chosen. How has your landscape of belief been shaped by the insights of others?
7. We rarely choose our neighbours. When Jesus tells the Parable of the Good Samaritan, he is confounding his listeners with a lesson in how to care for and regard 'others', or how to receive care from people we'd prefer not to associate with, or might even despise. What is that lesson for us today, and how can we keep relearning it?

Try some of these steps as a group and see how you get on. If you can walk even a few paces in somebody else's shoes, you might begin to understand their life and journey. Most people will thank you for that. Some may even return the favour.

Bibliography

Basset, L. (2006). *Holy Anger: Jacob, Job, Jesus*. London, Continuum.

Donovan, V. J. (1982). *Christianity Rediscovered: An Epistle From The Masai*. London, SCM Press.

Fanthorpe, U. A. (1995). *Safe As Houses: Poems*. Upton Cross, Liskeard, Cornwall, Peterloo Poets.

Festinger, L., H. W. Riecken and S. Schachter (1956). *When Prophecy Fails*. Minneapolis, University of Minnesota Press.

Foucault, M. and C. Gordon (1980). *Power/Knowledge: Selected Interviews And Other Writings, 1972–1977*. New York, Pantheon Books.

Fromm, E. (1973). *The Anatomy of Human Destructiveness*. New York, Holt, Rinehart and Winston.

Geertz, C. and R. Darnton (2017). *The Interpretation Of Cultures: Selected Essays*. New York, Basic Books.

Girard, R. and P. Gregory (1995). *Violence And The Sacred*. London, Athlone Press.

Gregory, D. (2004). *The Colonial Present: Afghanistan, Palestine, Iraq*. Malden, MA; Oxford, Blackwell Publishing.

Greider, K. (1996). 'Too Militant? Aggression, Gender and the Construction of Justice'. *Through The Eyes Of Women: Insights For Pastoral Care*. J. Moessner. Minneapolis, Fortress Press.

Hahn, C. (1994). *Growing In Authority, Relinquishing Control: A New Approach To Faithful Leadership*. Washington DC, Alban Institute.

Haidt, J. (2012). *The Righteous Mind: Why Good People Are Divided By Politics And Religion*. London, Allen Lane.

Hardy, D. W. (1989). 'Theology Through Philosophy'. *The Modern Theologians: An Introduction To Christian Theology In The Twentieth Century*. D. F. Ford. Oxford, Basil Blackwell.

Harrison, B. W. and C. S. Robb (1985). *Making The Connections: Essays In Feminist Social Ethics*. Boston, Beacon Press.

Hervieu-Léger, D. (2000). *Religion As A Chain Of Memory*. Oxford, Wiley.

Hoffer, E. (1964). *The True Believer: Thoughts On The Nature Of Mass Movements*. New York, The New American Library.

Hopewell, J. F. (1987). *Congregation: Stories And Structures*. Philadelphia, Fortress Press.

Le Guin, U. K. (1992). *Dancing At The Edge Of The World: Thoughts On Words, Women, Places*. London, Paladin.

Lewis, C. S. (1949). *Transposition, And Other Addresses*. London, Geoffrey Bles.

Lukes, S. (1979). 'Power and Authority'. *A History Of Sociological Analysis*. T. B. Bottomore and R. A. Nisbet. London, Heinemann.

Menzel, J. (1985). *My Sweet Little Village*. Czech Republic, Ústřední půjčovna film: 98 minutes.

Midgley, M. (2004). *The Myths We Live By*. London, Routledge.

Midgley, M. (1984). *Wickedness*. London, Routledge.

Padzer, L. and M. Smith (1980). *Michelle Remembers*. New York, St Martin's Press.

Peterson, E. H. (1992). *Under The Unpredictable Plant: An Exploration In Vocational Holiness*. Grand Rapids: Leominster, Eerdmans; Gracewing.

Putnam, R. D. (2000). *Bowling Alone: The Collapse And Revival Of American Community*. New York; London, Simon & Schuster.

Robbins, J. (2004). *Becoming Sinners: Christianity And Moral Torment In A Papua New Guinea Society*. Berkeley, Calif.; London, University of California Press.

Robinson, J. A. T. (1963). *Honest To God*. London, SCM Press.

Robinson, M. (1994). 'Puritans and Prigs: An Anatomy of Zealotry'. *Salmagundi* (101/102): 36–54.

Said, E. W. (1978). *Orientalism*. New York, Pantheon Books.

Stoppard, T. (1972). *Jumpers*. London, Faber.

Taylor, J. V. (1972). *The Go-Between God: The Holy Spirit And The Christian Mission*. London, SCM.

Towler, R. (1984). *The Need For Certainty: A Sociological Study Of Conventional Religion*. London, Routledge & Kegan Paul.

Vidler, A. R. (1957). *Essays In Liberality*. London, SCM Press.

Weil, S. and J. M. Perrin (2000). *Waiting For God*. New York, HarperCollins.

CHRISTIAN ALTERNATIVE
BOOKS

THE NEW OPEN SPACES

Throughout the two thousand years of Christian tradition there
have been, and still are, groups and individuals that exist in
the margins and upon the edge of faith. But in Christianity's
contrapuntal history it has often been these outcasts and
pioneers that have forged contemporary orthodoxy out
of former radicalism as belief evolves to engage with and
encompass the ever-changing social and scientific realities. Real
faith lies not in the comfortable certainties of the Orthodox,
but somewhere in a half-glimpsed hinterland on the dirt track
to Emmaus, where the Death of God meets the Resurrection,
where the supernatural Christ meets the historical Jesus,
and where the revolution liberates both the oppressed and
the oppressors.
Welcome to Christian Alternative... a space at the edge where
the light shines through.
If you have enjoyed this book, why not tell other readers by
posting a review on your preferred book site.

Recent bestsellers from Christian Alternative are:

Bread Not Stones
The Autobiography of An Eventful Life
Una Kroll
The spiritual autobiography of a truly remarkable woman
and a history of the struggle for ordination in the Church of
England.
Paperback: 978-1-78279-804-0 ebook: 978-1-78279-805-7

The Quaker Way
A Rediscovery
Rex Ambler
Although fairly well known, Quakerism is not well understood.
The purpose of this book is to explain how Quakerism works as
a spiritual practice.
Paperback: 978-1-78099-657-8 ebook: 978-1-78099-658-5

Blue Sky God
The Evolution of Science and Christianity
Don MacGregor
Quantum consciousness, morphic fields and blue-sky
thinking about God and Jesus the Christ.
Paperback: 978-1-84694-937-1 ebook: 978-1-84694-938-8

Celtic Wheel of the Year
Tess Ward
An original and inspiring selection of prayers combining
Christian and Celtic Pagan traditions, and interweaving their
calendars into a single pattern of prayer for every morning
and night of the year.
Paperback: 978-1-90504-795-6

Christian Atheist

Belonging without Believing

Brian Mountford

Christian Atheists don't believe in God but miss him: especially the transcendent beauty of his music, language, ethics, and community.

Paperback: 978-1-84694-439-0 ebook: 978-1-84694-929-6

Compassion Or Apocalypse?

A Comprehensible Guide to the Thoughts of René Girard

James Warren

How René Girard changes the way we think about God and the Bible, and its relevance for our apocalypse-threatened world.

Paperback: 978-1-78279-073-0 ebook: 978-1-78279-072-3

Diary Of A Gay Priest

The Tightrope Walker

Rev. Dr. Malcolm Johnson

Full of anecdotes and amusing stories, but the Church is still a dangerous place for a gay priest.

Paperback: 978-1-78279-002-0 ebook: 978-1-78099-999-9

Do You Need God?

Exploring Different Paths to Spirituality Even For Atheists

Rory J.Q. Barnes

An unbiased guide to the building blocks of spiritual belief.

Paperback: 978-1-78279-380-9 ebook: 978-1-78279-379-3

Readers of ebooks can buy or view any of these bestsellers by clicking on the live link in the title. Most titles are published in paperback and as an ebook. Paperbacks are available in traditional bookshops. Both print and ebook formats are available online.

Find more titles and sign up to our readers' newsletter at
http://www.johnhuntpublishing.com/christianity
Follow us on Facebook at
https://www.facebook.com/ChristianAlternative